FORGOTTEN GODS

K. HERMAN BOUMAN
1874-1947

FORGOTTEN GODS

PRIMITIVE MIND FROM A TRAVELLER'S POINT OF VIEW

BY

K. HERMAN BOUMAN†

Late Professor of Psychiatry and Neurology, University of Amsterdam

INTRODUCTION BY

G. VAN DER LEEUW

Professor of Theology, University of Groningen

WITH A PORTRAIT AND 29 ILLUSTRATIONS

LEIDEN
E. J. BRILL
1949

PRINTED IN THE NETHERLANDS

CONTENTS

LIST OF ILLUSTRATIONS

INTRODUCTION

Professor K. Herman Bouman was one of the most prominent among the psychiatrists and neurologists of the Netherlands. His work and personality have been described by H. C. Rümke in *Psychiatrische en Neurologische Bladen*, 1941, 2. But his interests extended beyond the limits of his own subject. The study of the human mind led him on towards a most profound inquiry into all things pertaining to man, especially primitive man, his origins, his migrations, his art and religion.

The little book which I have the honour of introducing to the public is a collection of essays on Anthropology in its widest sense. But it is not merely that. It has an added charm and quality. Bouman, who of course could never be an anthropological field-worker, found a very original and successful way, not only of lending to his abstract studies in the fields of anthropology, comparative religion and the history of art, the vigour and freshness of things seen and heard, but also of penetrating as deeply as possible into man's circumstances in the past. He travelled. But he not only saw a large part of the world, he also saw some part of the past of Man. He went to the prehistoric sites of France and Switzerland, he traced ancient customs in England, he saw primitive life in Australia and America. And he tried to find the connection between things read and things still to be seen. He tried to live through some of the experience of primitive man.

Of what he achieved, the reader must be the judge. I, for one, wish to state that I have read his little book not only with the greatest pleasure, but also with the greatest profit. Only a student of the human mind, as Bouman was, could write about matters so remote in such a fashion that they seem to be quite near, — as they indeed are, for that matter. The wide learning, the profound insight of the author find adequate expression in his simple, clear, and lucid language. A book not only for the chosen few, but for everyone. I sincerely hope it will travel all over the world, exactly as its author did.

Groningen   G. VAN DER LEEUW

PREFACE

In this series of essays the author tries to account for his opinion regarding the origin of some customs and habits which he witnessed travelling over the world, among both cultured and uncultured peoples.

All the customs under consideration have this in common that they are of very ancient origin, have been in high esteem until the present day, and looked upon in one way or another as sacred actions. They nearly all strike us as alien elements in our modern range of conceptions. As far as they can still be found in our modern culture, they appear to be relics which can be traced back to prehistoric times, before the memory of man.

The results of archaeological investigations may be helpful in many respects to corroborate conceptions formed along other ways. It is, however, especially modern psychology which has given us a more profound insight into primitive mind, without a knowledge of which we cannot understand the development of human mentality from the beginning up to the present time. In primitive mind we have to look for the dawn of art and religion, both of which are deeply rooted in a long-forgotten past.

By means of our knowledge about primitive mind—perhaps the most valuable discovery psychology ever made—we are enabled to overcome some difficulties, to clear up controversial ideas, and to make the meaning better understood of these at first sight sometimes incomprehensible customs which may otherwise seem meaningless or even absurd.

Out of that very remote past there have come to us the hazy forms of deified personages and mystic rulers, and vague rumours of gods now nameless and forgotten, but once the bearers of Supreme Power in the long-since vanished Pantheon at the dawn of mankind. Sometimes we can perceive only the faint echoes of their mighty power and glorious fame in myths or traditional ceremonies and in religious customs, as far they have been modified and adopted by our modern culture, but are sometimes still felt as alien to our mind.

Living today under the shadow of an uncertain future, at a time when old and sacred traditions seem to totter, and even the Church has to defend itself against a clamorous neo-heathenism, it might seem that even the Gods are not immortal. Surveying, however, the religious conceptions from the primitive past to the present, we may be convinced of the immortality of true faith.

Amsterdam, 1942.

CHAPTER I

BULL-FIGHTS

1. THE SPECTACLE

There can be no doubt about the fact that the greatest treat to the population of Spain and Portugal is to see a bull-fight. It is equally certain that the man who is most honoured and adored by men and women throughout the country, is the torero or bull-fighter.

In every town, and in many of the larger villages, bull-fights are held at regular times, and nobody who is able to walk or stand stays at home on the afternoon when the sound of trumpets, indicating the beginning of the spectacle, invites everybody to the "plaza de toros", the arena or market-place, where "el toro" is to meet his fate.

Many days in advance the coming "corrida", or bull-fight, is made known to the entire population by printed proclamations, with portraits of the "matadores", and pictures of the bulls that are to take part in the fight.

When the great day comes the throng fills the street leading to the place where the great event is to take place. The arena is soon filled with clamorous people. A band plays popular songs, and everybody is excited. At last a gate opens, and through it the small band of toreros enters the ring. First come the espadas, or matadores, then the banderilleros, picadores and other servants as drivers. All are richly dressed in antique costumes, and the picture presented is one of dazzling colour.

As the band begins to play the national anthem, the first espada or toreador proceeds solemnly to the tribune of honour, where the high officials are sitting. There he salutes the president, and asks him to allow the fight to begin.

Trumpets sound, the crowd applauds, and the toreros walk solemnly round the entire arena amidst the cheers of the spectators. Suddenly a silence falls, for the trumpet calls the bull—waiting outside in its "toril" or pen—to enter the arena. Then the gates open and a furious bull leaps into the ring. Immediately the nerves of the spectators are strung to the highest pitch as the animal—

foaming at the mouth with rage—looks around in search of its adversaries.

Then the fight is on, and on both sides is the will to kill. It is a downright life-and-death struggle, which ends only when one of the opponents is killed. It is "the Death in the Afternoon" described many a time by historians and poets, pictured by artists, and worshipped by the people; a spectacle as old as history itself, and still in existence amid the civilisation of our 20th century.

In Spain the principal person in this sport is the espada, or matador: the foremost toreader, or bull-fighter. Having been first provoked by the picadores and banderilleros, who prick the animal's back with little pointed darts, and excited by scarlet mantillas, the bull becomes very furious. Then the enraged creature is a most dangerous enemy indeed, and woe to him who comes near.

At this moment the espada goes into action. Standing in front of his adversary, and armed only with a thin rapier, he awaits the moment when the bull charges. Then, standing between the menacing horns, he bends over the rugged head and thrusts his long rapier beside the backbone into the heart of the animal.

Only a very skilful fighter dare risk this position, even for a single moment. For, if the critical moment be wrongly chosen, or if he miss the heart, he cannot avoid being caught on the mighty horns of the brute and thrown into the air. Horribly wounded, he has to be carried off, in the meantime protected by his assistants against the fatal attacks of the infuriated animal. Many a famous toreador, conqueror in a hundred fights, has miserably lost his life in this way.

But if he succeeds in doing his dangerous work skilfully and in accordance with all the rules which a very old tradition strictly prescribes, the crowd, mad with joy, breaks out into wild cheers.

In many respects the fight is a fair one. For if the bull-fighter makes a mistake, does not act according to the rules, does not give the bull a fair chance, or blunders in some way, the whole crowd hisses and loudly voices its disapproval. He is held up to scorn, and may leave the ring only with dishonour.

Although in Spain the bull-fight is a serious affair to one at least of the parties concerned, elsewhere civilisation has softened this cruel practice. Thus, in southern France it is forbidden to kill the bull. On the other hand, the dangerous points of the horns are rendered harmless, or filed off. Though there is no great danger of serious accidents on either side, they nevertheless sometimes occur.

But in Portugal the spectacle still bears the features of the old days of glory, and is held in high esteem by the people. The character of the fight, however, differs greatly from that in Spain, because it is chiefly a game of elegance and dexterity for the wonderful horses specially bred and trained for the purpose. Whereas in Spain the horses are always wretched animals, doomed to be miserably sacrificed, the Portuguese horses are very beautiful and well-trained animals of a good breed. The rider is a nobleman, dressed in an antique costume of marvellous colour, and an excellent horseman. The clumsy movements of the heavy bull and the elegance of the splendid steed form a marvellous contrast as the latter entices the former to charge. It is a graceful game between the intelligent horse and the clumsy bull, and nobody can doubt which will be the winner and which the loser. The horse always outruns his opponent and avoids the horns in the nick of time.

But the fight is not finished after the horseman has thrown his last pair of banderillas, little darts with barbed points. Another fighter goes into action, this time a torero on foot and wholly unarmed. He is a man of Herculean stature, his simple dress is of very ancient design. He takes up a position in the centre of the arena, his arms crossed behind his back and, standing right in front of the bull, he awaits the charging animal. At the very moment when the bull is about to throw his enemy into the air, when his mighty head is on the point of crashing into the stomach of his opponent, the latter grasps the bull by the horns and presses the enormous head down towards the ground. Single-handed he breaks the power of the infuriated animal.

At the moment when the bull-fighter forces the bull's head downwards, both his arms round the horns, and his own head bending forwards upon the shaggy shoulders of the animal, his position is quite remarkable. If he were not a man of immense strength he would be thrown into the air, legs swinging, his head resting upon the shoulders of the bull. But as he is in fact a most powerful man, he manages, as a rule, to maintain his position.

It will be clear that for the spectators this dangerous and difficult action forms the climax of the whole performance. This particular bull-fighter is the hero of the crowd. He is carried off in triumph

on the shoulders of his colleagues as soon as the bull, now fully conquered, is led out of the ring. For in Portugal, as a rule, the bull is
not killed.

The different ways in which the bull-fight is practised in those
countries where it is still a popular performance, are due to the fact
that it is a survival of ancient traditions, which have been preserved
in varying degrees in different countries. It is said that the Moors of
Africa introduced this kind of sport into Spain, and that afterwards
it became a national sport. But it is certainly much older than the
time of the Moorish invasion. In fact, we have to go far back into
history to find the first traces of the bull-fight.

But not every feature in the original performance has been preserved up till our time. Many of them are lost for ever; others are
folkloristic "survivals" in various countries, and some are mere
"fossils", the original meaning of which nobody knows now.

Today it is a "spectacle" only, but once it was a religious cult.
In ancient times bull-fights had a deeper sense, and at the bottom
of all this lies a real human drama.

2. THE CULT

Long before the dawn of Hellenic civilization, a highly developed
and splendid culture flourished throughout the whole eastern Mediterranean world. With Crete as its centre, and the islands of the Aegean
and the shores of southern Greece as advance guards, this Minoan
culture sprang up during the second millennium B.C.

Its splendour is still to be seen in the ruins of Cnossus, Phaestus
and Mycenae. Isolated on the islands and for the greater part shut off
from the rest of the world, a cultured and artistic people lived for
many centuries in peace. Only on the continent were the palaces of
Mycenean rulers built into strongholds against invading raiders from
the north, but in Crete itself such palaces were wholly unprotected.

These Minoan kings in Creta must have been powerful rulers and
sacred personnages, virtually worshipped as divinities. Everything
we know of the Minoan people bespeaks wealth, prosperity and
artistic sense. Excavations of these palace ruins have revealed that
very seldom did sudden destruction by fire disturb this peaceful
society; earthquakes or dynastic revolutions may account for such
disasters.

It was not until the beginning of the first millennium B.C. that a

Doric invasion from the continent brought to a definite end this marvellous and amazing civilization, which shows many remarkable characteristics. One of them is the cult of a fabulous monster with the body of a man and the head of a bull: the Minotaur. It was supposed to be the offspring of the wife of Minos, the legendary king of Crete, son of Zeus and Europe.

Greek historians (Plutarch, for instance) tell us how Minos demanded seven Athenian youths and maidens every eight years, to be sent to Cnossus as a sacrifice to the Minotaur. When Theseus volunteered to go he slew the Minotaur and escaped from the Labyrinth with the help of Ariadne, daughter of Minos.

Legends have been woven round the personages of this drama, and it is by no means certain that Minos is an historical figure. More likely this word means "king", and Greek historians mistook the title for a proper name. The connection between the words Minos (king) and Minotaur (partly man and partly bull), also the mythical wedding between Pasiphaë, wife of Minos, and the fabulous monster, indicate without doubt a very close connection between the "king" and the "bull".

So far as regards historical tradition.

On the other hand, archaeology also has a word to say about this interesting problem. The ruins of the great palace at Cnossus were excavated a few decades ago by Sir Arthur Evans. This is what he found: a large and very complex building with halls, inner-courts, chambers, store-rooms and corridors, everything of exquisite splendour and beauty. The whole of it is so complicated that one might easily lose one's way, and it is obvious that this confusing and intricate building is actually the Labyrinth of the legend.

Among the objects of art bulls' heads and bulls' statues are frequently met with and bull-fights are often depicted on the walls. From all this we may conclude that bull-fights, as a ceremonial festival, were common in those early ages. Amid a crowd of spectators, consisting of richly dressed ladies seated on the foremost benches, and with tall gentlemen standing in the background, young men are trying to leap over the bull's head in such a way that they are caught by girls, standing with raised arms behind the animal.

The attitude of the young man is remarkable, and archaeologists call him the "Springer": head down, legs in the air (fig. 1). This particular attitude was in fact a well-known characteristic of Minoan art as early as about 1500 B.C. Several specimens in ivory of the Springer are familiar objects among the treasures of the Museum of Hiraklion, the modern capital of Crete (fig. 2). There also the restored frescos of the bull-fight are to be seen.

If, however, we study the position of the Springer on these restored frescos, we wonder how he can manage to maintain his position, even for a moment (fig. 3). There is something incomprehensible in this attitude. I cannot help concluding that the restoration of the plaster

Fig. 1. Bull-fights in Minoan times (1) *).

is at fault. We have to bear in mind that the excavators found the palace completely in ruins, the walls utterly destroyed, the bricks strewn on all sides, and the plaster scattered all over the ground in small pieces, many of them missing. The reconstruction must have been a difficult one indeed, far more difficult than an ordinary jigsaw puzzle. Only if one accounts for every movement of the Springer, his motions during the jump, and the subsequent positions of his body, is one able to reconstruct the plaster correctly. In my opinion Sir Arthur was mistaken on this point, and I believe that the position of the Springer (head down, legs swinging in the air) should be understood as the position of the Portuguese bull-fighter

*) See Bibliographical notes. The figures between brackets refer to the books there listed.

Fig. 2. The Springer (Cnossus, c. 1600 B.C.).
Ivory.

Fig. 3. Restored Fresco (Cnossus).

who has failed to press the bull's head down, and has been tossed into the air.

If I am right in this, we may see in the Minoan springer the toreador of ancient times. He had to perform the fatal jump in such a way that, after being thrown into the air by the bull's head, he is caught

Fig. 4. Supposed position of the "Springer".

by the maidens at the right moment after the somersault. If he makes a mistake, however, the sharp horns of the brute will finish him off at the same moment (fig. 4).

According to Plutarch, the youth was sacrificed to the Minotaur. Archaeology shows us how this was performed. The slender and unarmed lad of ancient Minoan times is nothing but the forerunner of the skilful swordsman in Spain, and of the strong and nimble bull-fighter in Portugal.

We may surmise that the tribute of seven Athenian youths and maidens had some connection with the renewal of the divine king's powers every eight years by sympathetic magic. Tradition says that they were shut up in the Labyrinth and devoured by the Minotaur. Archaeological investigation has yielded a further example of such sacrifice. Be that as it may, there were certainly different manners of sacrifice in the course of time. If sacrifice consisted in being roasted alive in a bronze image of a bull-headed man, as some writers report, it was identical with the way in which the Phoenicians and Carthagenians sacrificed their offspring to Moloch.

There is little doubt that, according to modern mythologists, Minotaur is a personification of Baal-Moloch of the Phoenicians— that cruel devourer of children—and that in some way this god was connected with the sun. The same can be said of Minos, and it is obvious that Minos and Minotaur are two aspects of the same mythical personage. Moreover, we can trace the ceremonial slaughter of the bull throughout the Mediterranean and Asia Minor. Thus for instance in the cult of Mithras, whose worship spread first throughout Persia and Mesopotamia, and who afterwards became the greatest antagonist of Christianity.

The slaying of the Minotaur by Theseus indicated—from this point of view—the abolition of such human sacrifices; it meant the advance of European civilization, as represented first by Hellas, and it was already the early dawn of coming Christianity.

3. THE SLAYING OF THE MAN-GOD

In the beginning of human history mankind roamed the earth, and for untold ages Man lived a purely nomadic life. In small family-groups these "food-gatherers" went from hunting-ground to hunting-ground, from water-hole to water-hole, gathering wild fruit and corn, eating every edible food they could possibly find.

In those remote times mankind is supposed to have been cheerful, happy and innocent, and the first written documents concerning life refer to that Paradise and the Golden Age. Modern archaeological and anthropological investigations, however, have revealed a somewhat different picture of human life during the Old Stone Age, before the dawn of civilization. Nevertheless this simple life entirely ended with the coming of the Neolithicum, when civilization really began.

"The creation of civilization was the most tremendous revolution in the whole course of human history", as Dr. G. Elliot Smith (2), the famous anthropologist, says in his book "Human History". From the beginning of the New Stone Age an amazingly complex organization sprang up where conditions were favourable.

Whether this complicated process first began in Egypt or in Mesopotamia is doubtful. But it certainly started at the end of the fifth or at the beginning of the fourth millennium on the banks of the Nile and the Euphrat-Tigris at about the same time. Today we have a fairly clear idea of the conditions that existed in Egypt at the beginning of the Neolithicum. In those remote times the Nile rose and fell every year in exactly the same way as it does today. The water began to rise in June and July, and in September it swelled to a mighty tide. From September till November the banks were inundated and, as the flood then sank, the soil was once more covered with fertile mud. After the flood the natural crop of wild barley grew here and there upon small patches on the banks. Food-gatherers came in the spring to harvest the corn, and went away again till the next year.

For countless ages this cycle of natural events was witnessed by primitive people. They came and went, feasted in spring and starved in autumn and winter. Human brain was even then in a state of development to associate the two facts: the rise of the river and the growth of the barley. But people could not foretell the rise, nor did they know how to inundate the barren soil, until some men of exceptional insight imitated the natural process, dug channels and invented a system of basin irrigations.

From that time on agriculture became possible. People were no longer compelled to wander away in summer-time, but were now enabled to remain settled all the year round; they abandoned nomadic life and began to till the soil.

Only one vital question remained. Those early Egyptians were compelled to study the habits of the river, its rise and fall, to count the days and the moons between subsequent inundations, and to prepare ditches and channels at the right time. They had to know the exact time of the coming flood. In short, they were in need of arithmetic and of a calendar.

Then some man of constructive thought, a real genius, observed how the flood came every year after a certain brillant star, Sirius (the Egyptians called it Sothis), appeared above the horizon a few minutes before sunrise in July, about the time of the summer-solstice.

This was exactly the time when the Nile-flood began in Central Egypt. Consequently he was able to foretell the rise of the river. He was the man who knew the right time to build ditches and channels, he knew when to sow and when to reap.

His knowledge made him a powerful ruler, and people believed him to be a God who controlled the forces of Heaven. All social co-operation depended on him and on him only. He was the actual Giver of Life, and he was believed to be the cause of the changes he had predicted. The coincidence of the rising of Sirius with the flood of the Nile was interpreted in terms of cause and effect. Hence the belief that human destiny is written in the constellations of the stars.

Historical tradition, as handed down by Plutarch, combines this whole period of dawning civilization into the "Age of Osiris". He it was who taught his people agriculture and art, gave them laws, instructed them to worship the gods, created the first State-system, and he himself was the first God.

As he was the Giver of Life to the land and to the seed which the inundation made fertile, he was the Corn-God, the Nile-God, he was the Creator and he was the State (in a much more absolute sense than Louis XIV, King of France, who merely boasted: "L'état c'est moi").

As long as he was alive and in good health his people could live in safety. Famine need not be feared, fertility of the crops and herds was ensured. But if he were to die, or his strength to fail, disaster would threaten the whole State. His sacred life, his divine powers and his precious strength had to be maintained and renewed at any cost.

The myth of Osiris, handed down to our days by Greek authors and confirmed by archaeological investigation, tells us of his death and resurrection. According to Diodorus Siculus, he was murdered by his brother Set, and mutilated and dismembered. His wife and sister Isis recovered all the parts of his body. She buried them in different cities in order that Osiris might be worshipped in many places and that his divine power might bring fertility to the soil and prosperity to the people. According to Egyptian accounts, the lamentation of the mourning Isis and her sister Nephtys aroused the sorrow of the sun-god Ra, who sent down Anubis. The latter, with the help of Thott, Horus and the two sisters, pieced together the body of the murdered God. Then Osiris came to life again, and thenceforth reigned as king over death in the other world. His tragic death and happy resurrection were celebrated in Egypt with dramatic rites every year. Sacred bulls, called Apis and Mnevis, were dedicated to Osiris, and it was ordained that they should be worshipped as gods in his place.

The story of Osiris is the oldest in human history, told and retold in the course of centuries in many different forms and languages. The death of the Man-God and his resurrection can be traced into later times. In Greece the stories of Dionysos, Adonis or Attis are mere variations of this theme. These echoes of the past have never wholly faded out in history.

This account of the early origin of primitive priest-kingship was necessary to understand the evolution in later years. We have now to turn our attention to Mesopotamia, and also to more modern times.

In his wonderful book "The Golden Bough" (5) Sir James George Frazer describes how the priest-king lived a dangerous life. As long as his strength lasted, he was worshipped by his people as a living god on earth, for fertility of the crops, of the herd, of the people itself depended only on him. But if the safety of the people—and even of the world—is bound up with the life of the Man-God —human incarnation of divinity as he is—then the utmost care for his life and strength is called for, out of regard for the mere existence of his people. But as these human divinities are nevertheless human beings, they grow old and feeble and at last they die.

Their worshippers have to meet that calamity as best they can, for the danger is a most formidable one. The priest-king must be killed as soon as he shows symptoms of weakness or failure, and his soul must be transferred to a vigorous successor at the right moment. The only way, indeed, to avoid a catastrophe is to put the king to death as soon as he shows signs of ill-health or failing strength.

The ritual slaying of the king is a very old story, and goes far back into the mists of prehistory. Excavations in modern times of royal tombs in Sumer, Elam, Nubia, Caucasus and China (Han dynasty), show the pompous graves of many a priest-king, killed by strangulation, suffocation or otherwise, surrounded by the whole court, servants and slaves, whose shattered skulls tell a grim story of how they followed their lord and master into the hereafter.

The custom prevailed until recent times. Dr. C. G. Seligman, the eminent ethnologist, tells of a tribe near the White Nile where the king is held in high, indeed religious, reverence, but nevertheless his people cherish "the conviction that the king must not be allowed to become ill or senile, lest with his diminishing vigour the cattle should sicken and fail to bear their increase, the crops should rot in the fields, and men, stricken with diseases, should die in ever increasing number".

Sir James Fraser, quoting the above-mentioned author, says: "But the attack on him could only take place with any prospect of success at night, for during the day the king surrounded himself with his friends and his body-guards, and an aspirant to the throne could hardly hope to cut his way through them and strike home. It was otherwise at night. For then the guards were dismissed and the king was alone in his enclosure with his favourite wives, and there was no man near to defend him except a few herdsmen, whose huts stood a short way off. The hours of darkness were therefore seasons of peril for the king. It is said that he used to pass them in constant watchfulness, prowling round his huts fully armed, peering into the blackest shadows, or himself standing silent and alert, like a sentinel on duty, in some dark corner. When at last his rival appeared, the fight would take place in grim silence, broken only by the clash of spears and shields, for it was a point of honour with the king not to call herdsmen to his assistance."

In the course of time many ways were found to avoid the regicide, or to soften it. One of these was to kill the king at the end of a fixed term, or to enthrone a temporary king for a few days, who was killed in his place. Sometimes the king's substitute was chosen from the same race as the king, and since no one could represent him in his divine character so well as a son, one of them (as a rule he would have a large harem and many sons) was executed in order that the king's life might be spared. But, in any case, there had to be a ritual slaying of the priest-king in such a way that his soul could be transferred into another human body, in order that no hiatus should occur during the reign of the divine ruler. We can still hear the echo of all this in our time: "le Roi est mort, vive le Roi".

There were other ways, too, of saving the life of the king and yet at the same time to be obedient to the sacred law. Phenomena of identification are common in primitive mind. So priest-kings were often identified with other sacred things as the Sun, the Moon, the Stars, the River, or some animal.

The domestication of cattle is closely connected with the beginning of agriculture. The discovery of the fact that cow's milk could be used as food for human beings impressed primitive people as a most startling mystery. The Cow came to be regarded as a real foster-mother, and was called the Divine. Cow, the Mother of Mankind, in Egypt afterwards known as Hathor, the mother of Horus.

This process of syncretism went further until the Moon and the Sky were combined with the Cow. Also the Ox, draught-animal of the plough and tiller of the land, was worshipped. Above all, however, the Bull was venerated as a symbol of strength and fertility. It became a sacred animal and was identified with the king, whose physical strength and sexual fertility were of vital importance to the whole people. Especially in Asia Minor the bull frequently represented the king, and was therefore a common substitute on the day of his ritual slaying.

We have mentioned above how sacred bulls were dedicated to Osiris. Until the Roman conquest sacred bulls were sacrificed after a fixed term, drowned in the sacred spring, and interred in pompous tombs, which are still to be seen as "Serapaeums" in Egypt, for instance.

Priests formally announced the day of sacrifice to the bull, worshipped during its life as a god. Wreathed with flowers, it was solemnly led to the public place so that everybody could bear witness to the sacred deed. There it was shown to the people, and crowned with gaudy ribbons. Games and ceremonial festivals were also given in its honour. Sometimes it was also held up to ridicule, as was the custom when the king's substitute was a slave, a mock-king for a few days, finally to be sacrificed.

The slaying of the Man-God, already reduced to a cult in the second millennium, became a spectacle only after the coming of Christianity, and is today still a far-away echo of that human drama which is as old as civilization itself.

One wonders how much of it can be traced in that sacred story with which Christianity begins: the Via Dolorosa, the death and resurrection of the Saviour: Jesus Nazarenus, Rex Judaeorum.

CHAPTER II

ON SANCTUARIES

At the corner of a picturesque piazza in Rome, in the shadow of the antique mausoleum of the deified Augustus, there is one of the many churches dedicated to the Virgin. This sanctuary differs little from any other church in the centre of the Eternal City, but it has a remarkable name: "Santa Maria sopra Minerva".

There is history in this name. It expresses the fact that in classical days this temple was dedicated to another deity, and it reveals that Christians built a new sanctuary on its ruins. There is no direct connection between these two deities at all, nor between the two creeds. In many respects the daughter of Zeus was in fact the antithesis of the Holy Virgin. Thus the connection seems to exist in the chronological order only. After Christianity was proclaimed by Constantine the Great under the triumphal arch that still bears his name, the old pagan temple was dedicated to Mary, as were many others.

In fact, there was hardly any necessity to demolish the whole building. The statue of the pagan deity had merely to be destroyed, the antique cella pulled down and a brick wall erected round the colonnade. That done, a cross had to be set up and some emblem of one of the saints had to be painted on the wall—and the new cult had its home.

If one were to scrape the plaster from the wall one might observe on the bricks the stamp of some Roman factory of the last centuries before the Christian era. Perhaps one may detect somewhere in the mortar of the foundations some excellent piece of fine marble statuary or other evidence of wonderful antique workmanship. Nearly all the materials for the building came from the old temple. In short, the Christian church is chiefly a rebuilding of the sacred house erected to the worship of one of the Gods of the Olympus.

This is no exception. On the contrary, it is in fact the rule with regard to many an old Christian church—and not in Rome only. The San Clemente, for instance, is another and even more striking case in point. Here at least three different temples have been built one on top of the other, and—which is more surprising—all three are still partly in existence: the Christian church uppermost, then the lower church (once the house of the Saint himself, as the third successor to St. Peter), and deep under the ground an old sanctuary, probably of the republican period, with a Mithraic chapel.

Many other remarkable examples of this phenomenon are to be found everywhere in Rome. Only a few exceptions can be brought forward. Thus, for instance, the basilica of San Giovanni in Laterano, the "Mother of all churches", has been built on the ruins of an antique thermae of the patrician Lateran Palace. Although the world-famed San Pietro with its huge colonnade, the largest church in Christendom, was erected over the grave of the Apostle Peter, this place received its sanctity from this fact only. For, before the first Pope was buried here, this place was the scene of very profane affairs, such as a circus of Nero.

Striking examples of successive cultures with their accompanying religions being superimposed one on top of the other are to be found all over the world. Everywhere in Greece and Italy one may find evidence of this process. Culture succeeded culture in the course of time, and the remains of untold ages formed layer upon layer. Old buildings fell to ruins at last, but the ruins were never completely removed. Every following generation built its temples, houses, or fortifications, with the building materials found on the very spot.

During the long period of the Middle Ages the ancient fora and palaces of the Emperors were veritable mines of marble for the people to build new houses with. Or—a more simple procedure—they lived in those old buildings and made them into strong fortresses. The Colossea in Roma, Verona, Nîmes, Arles, and in so many other towns, were impregnable strongholds in Merovingian and Carolingian times. Even nowadays a large town like Spalato (i.e. "palazzo") is entirely built within one immense Roman palace.

With regard to sacred places in general, it is especially noticeable how holiness clings to a place once sanctified for some reason. When occasion offers, one can sometimes trace sacred places in the history of mankind as far back as the beginning of human life on earth. A few examples may be given here.

On the top of the mountain that overlooks Florence there once stood the Etruscan town of Fiesole. The original town disappeared after its destruction during the wars with the Roman Republic. In the early Middle Ages a new town was founded in the valley, on the banks of the Arno, which town is now called Firenze. Since that time, especially during the Renaissance, its edifices were constructed with the marble and the columns of old Fiesole. Even nowadays this marble-mine is not quite exhausted, and where formerly stood the Etruscan town, modern Fiesole is still in existence. A beautiful little church, dedicated to San Francisco, stands on the top of the mountain, and has been built partly on old remains of Roman temples and partly on the foundations of a Roman theatre. All these Roman ruins in their turn cover the remains of very old Etruscan temples and altar-bases. Undermost, one can observe "cyclopean" walls built of extraordinarily big stone blocks, which fortifications were already in existence before the first Etruscan immigration came from the east. Under these cyclopean stones a neolithic layer of implements and fragments of pottery is to be found, and it is almost certain that there are still older layers under this neolithic one before the virgin soil is reached.

Another example, San Luca, is a world-famed sanctuary, near Bologna. An immense cathedral on the top of the mountain overlooks the entire country and the plain of the river Po. Nowadays it is a place of pilgrimage for all Christendom. A picture of the Holy Virgin and Child performing miracles (without doubt an old Byzantine icon, though ascribed to San Luca himself), forms an attraction for cripples and sick persons of every kind, who believe they can be cured by touching the Holy Image. This reputation for healing in curable diseases is much older than Christianity itself. In fact, this sanctuary was already in existence and constituted a place of pilgrimage in Etruscan days, and even long before that time. Its origin goes back to the first settlements of very primitive people in the fertile plains of northern Italy in the unknown course of prehistoric times.

From these and similar observations we may conclude that there are "holy places" in the history of mankind, and that successive cults and religions simply took possession of such places. The name of the divinity, or the Saint, is merely accidental, and changes according to the ruling cult.

Sometimes the denominating "saint" appears to bear a name not registered in the official series of biblical personages, apostles and martyrs of the Christian church. In such cases it is usually a local name of some deity adopted by the church in the early Christian age.

I once saw a wonderful example of adoption of this kind in
Rocamadour, Dordogne, France. A complex of four or five churches
on the top of a mountain, high above the little valley, has been a place
of pilgrimage from time immemorial (fig. 5). The local clergy glory
in the fact that Rocamadour is much older than Lourdes, and they

Fig. 5. Church at Rocamadour, built against the
rock-wall of the ancient "abri sous roche".

assert that the Holy Image in their churches performs more and
greater miracles than in the rival "cave of Lourdes". All these Rocamadour churches have been constructed in such a way that one of
the four walls consists of the living rock itself. As the rock
is consequently part of the building, and the worshippers send up
their prayers to the Holy Virgin, whose image is attached to the
solid rock-wall, it is obvious that the rock is the principal object of
worship. Strangest of all, however, is the fact that the statue of the
Virgin is as black as a negro, and that the Child is inky black as
well. Such "Black Marys" are no exception in many European

countries. They always indicate the extraordinary antiquity of the sanctuary. It is at least probable that the origin of a sacred place like this can be traced as far back into the history of mankind as the last period of the Old Stone Age. Rocamadour may help to prove this theory. For it is certain that the rock-wall of the modern churches there forms the interior of a real "abri sous roche", and is therefore the back wall of a prehistoric cave of the Old Stone Age.

At one time the primitive hunters of palaeolithic times inhabited this cave, buried their chieftain in the soil and, that done, left the place alone for ever, as they believed it to be haunted and "taboo".

Fear and worship are different aspects of a single emotion. The word "sacer" in Latin still has this double meaning. The grave of the primitive "king" became a place of worship for ever. But successive generations came to sacrifice to the spirit of the "Old Man" buried there. Thus a local saint was born, a "genius loci", and became the performer of miracles. In course of time a cult arose, priests took possession of the place, and a sanctuary was erected. New generations and new creeds came and went—the Old Man stayed (only changing his name from time to time), and developed from a spirit to a divinity. As Christianity came to power the pagan spirit was adopted as a Christian saint. But the black spectre of the dead man incorporated in the black statue still bears, in our days, the features of the original.

Sometimes, as in Rocamadour, the bones of the Old Man were dug up. In the twelfth century the priests found a skeleton there at the bottom of the old abri. They believed they had found the "grave" of St. Amadeus, the local saint of the legend. Now his sacred bones are kept in the reliquary under the altar, and are the object of adoration and the source of miracles. But that sacred skull in the reliquary might bear all the characteristics of a representative of that ancient Cro-Magnon race that lived at least 50,000 years ago in the centre of France.

When the first men came into Europe they believed in immortality. They feared the chieftain even after his death. Therefore he was buried and a big stone cast upon his grave to make it impossible for him to rise again. After the burial the little family-group fled, and came back again for offerings only.

As to their belief in immortality they were right—for the "Old Man" is still alive today! The place where he was once buried is now a famous centre of pilgrimage, and his spirit performs miracles.

CHAPTER III

THE LONELY SHRINE

1. BURIED PAST

Standing upon the bridge which crosses the little river Vézère, near the village of Les Eyzies-de-Tayac, Dordogne, one finds oneself amidst a typical rural landscape in the centre of France. The picturesque river, winding through a narrow valley, is surrounded by steep limestone rocks, real falaises, towering 200 to 300 feet above the stream and overgrown with shrubs and moss. Here and there along the bank of the river stands a farm-house in the shelter of the rocks, and farther away in the distance the roofs of the houses of some other little village may be perceived. No other sounds but the creaking of a farm-cart along the road, the voice of a man urging on his old horse, or the call of a boy driving his cows to pasture, disturb the solitude of this quiet and peaceful world. The road along the river-bank is mostly deserted and the lonely passers-by are nearly all inhabitants of the villages and farm-houses in the valley, coming from, or going to, their daily work. When they pass beneath the little shrine erected halfway up the slope of the rocks, in which the image of some Christian Saint, the Virgin, or a Crucifix has been placed by their forbears, they never omit to look up at that lonely sanctuary, standing forgotten amidst the flowers of the pasture or the grapes of some small vineyard, and to lift their hats while muttering an "Ave Maria". From daybreak until the sound of the Angelus bells, peace and quiet reign all over the valley of the Vézère.

There was, however, a time when conditions were different. For long ago, at the dawn of mankind, this very valley was the scene of intense human activity, and teeming with life.

Standing on the bridge, we are in fact surveying a panorama of rock-shelters, "abris sous roche", where prehistoric man lived during the glacial periods and in the time between two such successive phases of severe cold, when the glaciers of far-away high mountains covered the greater part of Europe. The remains of early culture, long ago hidden by the fallen mass of debris from the rocks around, but now excavated by modern archaeologists, have been found in such enormous quantities on the slopes of the rocks, in the caves, and all along the banks of the rivier, that the conviction has gained ground that a most important centre of very early cultural life was concentrated in the valleys of this country, and that Les Eyzies may be termed one of the most important prehistoric "capitals".

The reason is not far to seek. In palaeolithic times few places were naturally suited to human habitation, a great part of the continent being covered with ice. Because of the severe cold man sought shelter under the overhanging rocks and in the caves, and it was especially in this part of France that the conditions for this kind of shelter were favourable. The sedimentary limestone, which is found here, intersected as it was in early geological times by mighty streams which furrowed their bed for untold ages into the relatively soft limestone, in this way caused many deep valleys. The running water, scalloping out the steep side of the rocks, formed at length at their base hollows and caves of every size and extent. Here and there the excavating stream disappeared into the ground and, running great distances under the surface, formed subterranean lakes and streams, passing in their course a series of wonderful corridors and halls.

In these sheltered places palaeolithic man lived during the long glacial epochs. Opening towards the south and the south-west, these "abris sous roche" were more or less protected from the cold winds. During the inter-glacial periods the climate had been warmer, sometimes even rather hot. Then early palaeolithic man lived in the open, in front of the overhanging rocks, fishing along the river-banks, or hunting on the tablelands. But as the glaciers began to descend anew from the mountain-tops and gradually advanced towards the lower valleys and plains, man was driven into the deeper parts of his rock-shelter. And when the icy tongues of the glaciers reached their farthest point, man sought refuge entirely in the caves. This, at least, was the fate of Old Stone Age man in Europe.

During those very long epochs the development from animal into man came about, slowly but gradually. Of some of these successive degrees of evolution we have found scanty remains to testify to primitive man's culture, and in this way we are able more or less to trace his remarkable psychical development.

Under the influence of atmospheric changes, climate and erosion, the appearance of the earth altered little by little. Forests arose during the warmer periods, and gave place to tundras in the cold ones. Rivers grew to mighty streams when the glaciers melted away, and after that became brooks again. Rocks, time-worn and weather-beaten, were demolished and fell to pieces, blocking the streams and thus causing lakes to be formed. The fallen stones, converted into boulders, gravel and sand, were finally removed by the rivers, in this way forming new land elsewhere.

In the centre of France, especially in the country round Les Eyzies, the limestone erosion facilitated the forming of rock shelters and caves, thus making conditions here favourable for habitation. Primitive man found plenty of space in the many shelters of these narrow and wind-protected valleys to shield himself from the rough climate.

Today practically all these abris and caves have disappeared, because they have been filled up in the course of time by fallen stones and debris from the cliffs above, and were in this way swept from sight. Now a steep slope rises up from the river nearly half-way to the rim of the plateau, consisting of fallen stones and gravel. In the course of time this limestone debris covered the contents of the abri, including all the remains of primitive culture.

Careful excavations in recent years have brought to light some of the implements and bones which had withstood the wear and tear of time, and it is from the results of modern archaeological investigations that we are enabled to reconstruct in rough lines the physical and psychical structure of the long since vanished races that once peopled the centre of Europe in the Old Stone Age (6, 7).

In the old dwelling-places we can distinguish the different layers on which the abris are now built up. Undermost we find the oldest, where the most primitive human beings have left their traces, and as later races came and went, others layers were deposited one on top of the other. An ideal section through one of these rock-shelters gives us, so to say, a stratographic survey of the history of mankind from the beginning until modern times (fig. 6).

As far as the most ancient cultural epochs—Chellean and Acheulean—have left any remains, these are to be found in front of the rocks, among the boulders of the river-bed and upon the plateau, for in those very remote times, between the second and the third glacial period, the temperature was high, and forests covered the land. As a matter of fact, we know very little about the culture of those races, which, though undoubtedly human, nevertheless were in the earliest phase of evolution. A few rough-hewn stone implements and some questionable skull-bones are almost all we have to base our conclusions upon.

We are better informed respecting the Neanderthal-race, which belonged to the Mousterian culture, living at the close of the third glacial epoch and during the whole of the last inter-glacial period.

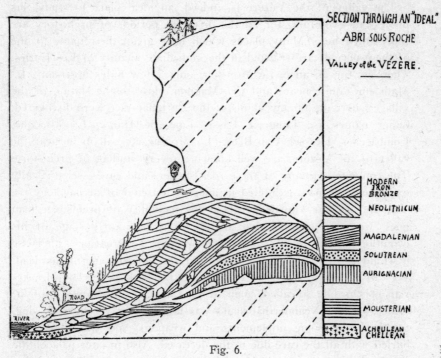

Fig. 6.

As long as the climate was warm enough they lived outside the rock-shelters, but as the glaciers drew nearer they retired under the overhanging cliffs. They, too, were still a poorly developed human race.

Then, at the opening of the last glacial period, a new race appeared in Europe, now for the first time the same as that to which modern man belongs: the Cro-Magnon man, who lived during the period called Aurignacian.

The dwelling-places of these races are to be found deep in the caves, as are those which belong to the cultural phases known as the Solutrean and Magdalenian, for all these different races inhabited Europe during the last Ice-Age.

As Neolithicum began, representatives of new races entered Europe, occupying the abandoned homes of palaeolithic man. But as the glaciers melted away and the climate grew warmer, these newcomers settled down further outside the rock-shelters.

In the abris, where conditions are favourable for such investigations, we may find the whole series of layers, each representing one of the periods of culture that have been named.

The valley of the Vézère is, indeed, an ideal place to study this process of evolution, for all the different periods of prehistory are represented here. Many places which have given their name to one of these periods are situated in the immediate vicinity of Les Eyzies. There is, for instance, Le Moustier, only a few miles upstream; La Madeleine, quite near; and Cro-Magnon, close to the station of the village where the famous skulls of the Aurignac race were discovered. Other names as: Laugerie Basse, Laugerie Haute, La Micoque, Combarelles, Laussel, Cap-Blanc, La Mouthe etc., all in or near the valley of the Vézère, are well known to every student of prehistory. The contents of many of these rock-shelters and caves, scientifically excavated, are now exhibited in many a museum of archaeology.

As far as our knowledge about the mentality of prehistoric man goes, we may presume that already in a very early stage of his evolution he had some vague conception of a hereafter. Otherwise it would be difficult to understand why he buried some of his dead. We can even find traces of a funeral as far back as the late Mousterian epoch. The so-called "man of La Chapelle aux Saints", for instance,—a real Neanderthal man—was laid in a grave expressly dug, together with some implements and weapons, and was apparently buried with all the care due to the deceased. Also in later palaeolithic times—Aurignacian and Magdalenian—many graves indicate that physical death was not considered the end, but that the soul was believed to continue its existence in the other world.

The way the dead have been found lying in their graves demonstrates that careful attention was paid to position and direction when interring the corpse. We cannot escape the impression that the corpse was often intentionally mutilated, head and limbs being buried separately, or covered with big stones, or—as was the custom until the end of Neolithicum—bound with ropes; in short, that every precaution was taken to prevent the dead from rising again.

On the other hand, primitive man tried to appease the dead by giving them their personal belongings and everything they might possibly need on the long journey beyond the tomb.

Hate, fright, envy and—above all—the intense fear that the dead man might come back, were presumably the motives that led very primitive man to treat the corpse in this way, subtler feelings not yet having been born in his mind (8, 9).

All we do know about the structure of that most primitive group, the horde, points to the fact that the small family-group was despotically ruled by an older man, who tyrannized, pitilessly and egotistically, his wives and offspring, undisputed master as he was, and who could only maintain his power by brute force. But as soon as his strength began to fail, his sons killed him, and fought amongst themselves the battle for supremacy. They had good reason indeed not to want the old tyrant back to take the lead again. As his leadership, however, depended only on his strength, courage and power, his offspring wished most of all to preserve these precious gifts from destruction and loss. Thus his sons were compelled to eat the body of the old family-father, absorbing in this way the power that had caused them to suffer so cruelly, and thus preserving it for themselves.

According to modern psychologists this scene, and the burden of sin originating from it, still occupies the background of our mind, emerging symbolically in some form or other. It is the "scena" of the Old Stone Age, where the flesh and blood of the slain father, their creator, was eaten by his offspring in the course of a communal meal—a palaeolithic "Lord's Supper" (15).

After the corpse—or what was left of it—had been interred, the burial-place—now taboo—had to be avoided by the tribe, and often the inhabitants of the cave abandoned their home for ever. When later on newcomers settled down, tradition kept the story of the ghost alive. And when in the course of time a primitive religion had sprung up, born of a magic past, the "genius loci" became transferred into some deity or saint. Up to our day some of these ancient places are still known by the name of a local·saint, now adopted by the Church. Some of them have obtained a famed reputation for healing diseases, others have passed from the memory of man.

In the valleys of the centre of France we may find somewhere on the slope of the rocks above the river a little shrine, lonely and forgotten amidst the bushes and vines, containing a simple image of the Virgin, a Saint, or a Crucifix. As a pious tradition maintains, the god has stood there from the beginning.

2. "MADONNA NERA"

It is a remarkable fact that among the many ancient votive-statues in central Europe, Spain and Italy, a few have come to us picturing the Holy Virgin as black as a negro. We may presume that their number must have been greater formerly, and that those which are still in existence today are only a few out of many that once existed. Such a "Madonna Nera" always has an age-old reputation, and very often its home is a place of pilgrimage or of world-famed processions. Very often these statues are famed for curing diseases, emanating in some way or other a fluidum, some mystic, magic power, which—life-giving as it is—is able to restore health and to bring happiness and good fortune.

Though this point has sometimes—though very seldom, for that matter—been a subject of study, scarcely any enquiry has been made, as far as I know, into the origin and significance of such black goddesses, the question having been looked upon chiefly from a descriptive point of view.

Now we have to bear in mind that what are usually called Madonna Nera, Vierge Noire, Schwarze Muttergottes—all votive-pictures representing the Holy Virgin with the Child—are Byzantine icons, which came from the east during or after the Crusades in the XI and XII centuries (fig. 7). They were brought to Western Europe because of their reputation for performing miracles. Originally they were not "black" at all, but became so, the pigment having altered under atmospheric influences in the course of time. These Byzantine icons are traditionally ascribed to St. Luke, the patron saint of early Christian painters, in this quality thus succeeding Daedalus, who, according to classic tradition, was the painter of holy images in Hellas.

According to some authors these medieval votive-pictures served to supply the place of vanished pagan idols. Long before Christianity black idols, representing some deity, had existed. Pausanias mentions an "Aphrodite melaina" and "Demeter melaina" in Phigalia, and also the statue of "Artemis Ephesia" represented a black goddess; while there were others as well in Hellas, as Ceres and Cybele. In Egypt, too, there was a special cult of a "black Isis" (whose priests were tonsured).

Though all this is rather vague and confusing we may presume that such black images originate from a very ancient chthonic goddess,

representing the deified Earth, a female deity personifying fecundity
and prosperity, who, according to the ruling pantheon, took the shape
of Isis, Demeter, Aphrodite or the Virgin. As "Madonna Nera" she
survives in the adoration of the Virgin, a most venerated and
sacred deity (10).

Fig. 7. Byzantine Madonna (XI century)
The picture itself is covered with a golden
plate, richly decorated with pearls and
precious stones; only the heads and hands
of the original picture are visible.

Apart from the above-mentioned Byzantine icons, however, there
are at present still a few real black statues of a female deity to
prove that the ancient black pagan idols are not wholly extinct.
These are most probably remnants of the many that once existed
(11, 12, 13). Some of them form a centre of pilgrimage, and are
held in high esteem throughout the world. We may mention here, for
instance: "Madonna del Monte Virgine" (near Naples, the so-called
"Mamma Schiavona"); "Madonna di Crotone" (Calabria); "Madonna
di Loreto"; "Madonna at Monserrato" (Spain); ' Madonna at Einsie-

deln"; "Madonna at Wildkirchli" (St. Gallen); "Madonna at Altöt-
ting" (Bavaria); "Madonna at Rocamadour" (France). One of the
three Madonnas at "Les Saintes Maries" (Camarque, France) is St.
Sara, a black Madonna, patroness of the Gipsies, who every year
on the 20th of May come from all parts of the world to worship
their special Saint. In the crypt of the cathedral of Chartres there was
a "Vierge Noire" up to the Middle Ages, but having been destroyed,
it is now replaced by a modern statue.

Fig. 8. Rock-shelter sanctuary, with procession
(picture by Joost de Momper).

After all this we need not discuss the great antiquity of these
female deities any longer, but may point to the fact that we always
find them in close connection with particular geographical conditions.
Very often the foundations of the church, where they are now
worshipped, rest upon, or are built over, a cave in the rock ground,
as at Chartres, and sometimes the crypt of the church itself is in-
dubitably a real "abri sous roche". Or one of the walls of the
sanctuary may be the bare rock, and the worshippers utter their
prayers facing the rock against which the black statue is placed, as,
for instance, at Rocamadour. Sometimes we may find the sanctuary
far away from any habitation, in an out-of-the-way place in the wild
open country, high up against the side of a rock, as, for instance, at

Wildkirchli, where the abri is still clearly recognizable (fig. 8, fig. 9).

As regards the Virgin in the simple shrine in the valley of the Vézère, we see there presumably the last trace of the black goddess, who has stood there from the beginning of time.

Fig. 9. Wildkirchli, near Appenzell, Switzerland.
Rock-shelter sanctuary; the old "abri sous roche"
is clearly recognizable.

There is, after all, abundant evidence concerning a close connection between the votive-statue and the original abri, so that we may conclude that they have belonged together since palaeolithic times.

Why the statue is black is difficult to say. There is no reason whatsoever to suppose (as some authors suggest) that the black colour has a symbolical meaning as, for instance, the mystical birth of the Virgin, or Her sufferings on behalf of humanity; for the black goddess existed long before Christianity. It is better to approach the question from another side, perhaps, though we have to confess that all this is merely speculative. Idols, as is apparent, bear the form and characteristics of the people who made them; thus they resemble human beings. It might therefore be that the black idols came from a dark-skinned people. This is not mere guesswork, for it is highly probable that in palaeolithic times at least part of the population of Europe was of a marked negroid type, as the Grimaldi skeletons, excavated in the "Grotte des Enfants", Mentone, may prove (if Prof. Boule is right in this supposition). For the present, however, the question of the dark colour can hardly be decided with certainty.

3. THE ANCIENT MOTHER

In the Old Stone Age the Pantheon was not yet extensive, and embraced but a few deities.

The Old Man, slain by his sons and feared even after his death, became in the course of time the deified Vengeance. His inevitable fate hung continually like Damocles' sword above the head of each of his successors in turn. The remembrance of this deed of violence perpetually haunted them, renewed as it was, again and again, with each new change of power in the group. The threat of revenge on the part of the deceased forbears created a hostile world beyond the tomb, which had to be appeased as much as possible. A burden of sin originated from this deed, the original sin, creating a perpetually guilty conscience. We can still hear the echo in much later times, for does not the Old Testamentary Jahwe say: "Vengeance is Mine"?

Besides this male element another has come into being, this time a female one. Man depending on the fertility of surrounding nature for mere existence, food was the most important factor. Not being able rationally to influence the increase of game and fish, or the yield of fructiferous plants, primitive man resorted to irrational means, namely to magic. In his immediate surroundings, within his own family and tribe, he saw the birth of new life. The wonder of Motherhood amazed him, and he saw in the child-bearing mother the Giver of Life. The magic of Motherhood found expression in the making of female figurines, used as amulets to protect the living. In the pregnant woman and in child-birth he saw the means to influence the vegetation around him.

Female idols with exaggerated sexual characteristics are among the first objects of culture we know of. In the Middle Aurignacian, which is famous for its realistic pictures on rock-walls, we find small female statuettes, round plastics, commonly called "Venus". They have been found in many parts of Europe and Asia, from the Indus to the Nile, in Asia Minor, Siberia, and south-west Europe, and are exceptionally interesting because they represent the unclothed human form in a most realistic way. These figurines are made of stone, bone or ivory; when they were made of other material, namely wood or ceramic, they seldom withstood the wear and tear of time. Though these human forms are probably hyperstylized, we can nevertheless observe qualities which may point to racial characteristics, such as steatopygia and woolly hair, quite in the same way as we see them today in some African races. This fact also favours the supposition that some palaeolithic races were of negroid type.

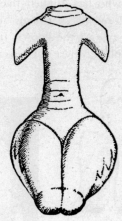

Fig. 10. Ancient Nubian amulet, representing both a woman and a cowrie-shell.

Modern archaeological investigations have made it probable that these female idols belong to a palaeolithic hand-axe culture, which at least already implies a very primitive agriculture (7). In Mesopotamia and Egypt we may presumably see the origin of this culture. When agriculture developed, these idols spread over wider areas, having been ever since an attribute of village-cultures of the whole Neolithicum. They persisted even in much later times, as we shall see.

Originally the specifically female characteristics were purposely emphasized, special attention being paid to the breasts and the abdomen, while legs, arms and face were omitted or but vaguely indicated. The lines of abdomen and hips together form a figure which can be seen in about the same fashion in the lines of a cowrie-shell, and thus the model of a cowrie may be so fashioned that it looks a caricature of a woman's abdomen. Dr. G. Elliot Smith (2), the famous anthropologist, discussing this subject, even describes an old Nubian amulet where the female idol and the cowrie are combined (fig. 10). "The cowrie", he says, "was originally the symbol of the 'one entrance into life', a belief that is still widespread among both uncultured and cultured peoples". Thus the cowrie, having become an amulet, is used as currency among primitive tribes at the present day.

In this way a Vegetation goddess was received into the Pantheon of the Mammoth-hunters of late palaeolithicum. In our time a great many of such female idols have been excavated. According to Dr. Absolon, who has studied these idols especially and excavated some very interesting specimens himself in Moravia, there is some difference in the style of the known figurines, 91 in all, of this kind, according to the place where they were excavated, but they nevertheless form a unit.

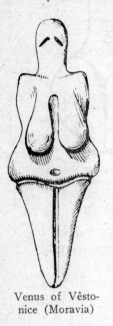  

Venus of Vêsto-   Venus of Lespugue   Venus of Willendorf (Austria)
nice (Moravia)   (Haute Garonne)

Fig. 11. Palaeolithic Idols.

A few of these female idols may be mentioned here. The "Venus of Willendorf", among the first ever excavated, represents a fat, steatopygous woman, with enormous breasts and woolly hair; the "Venus of Vêstonice", likewise with exaggerated female characteristics; the "Venus of Brassempouy", also called "la poire"; the "Venus impudique" of Laugerie Basse, and many others now well-known to every student of prehistory (fig. 11).

With the spreading of agriculture in early Neolithicum these female idols found their way over the greater part of Europe and Asia. Though the original idea prevailed, the form changed and developed.

To emphasize motherhood, a child held in the arm or sucking at the breast became more and more an indispensable attribute. When later on the history of man could be put into writing and prehistory ended, we meet for the first time a name for this goddess: Innima (Inanna), with the Sumerians; Istar (i.e. the goddess *par excellence*) with

Fig. 12. Isis and Horus (Karnak, about
1000 B.C.).

the Semites, goddess of vegetation, fecundity, birth and love; Antum, with the Babylonians, personifying the Earth (14). From that time onwards we can trace the Mother-Child image up to our day. In Egypt it was Isis — the wife and sister of the Corn-God Osiris—with the Child Horus who became the traditional bearer of fecundity, life-giving and child-birth. She wore the sacred Egyptian Sun-disk between Apis-horns on her head, as a symbol of her Supreme Power (fig. 12). When at last Christianity came, it accepted, in a final syncretism of all the sacred conceptions of the time, the Mother-Child image of old as well. The sun-disk between the Apis-horns disappeared and changed into the Graeco-Roman circle, or Coptic halo, behind the head. It was from this image that the Byzantine Madonna originated.

With the adoption of the image, however, young Christendom raised the sacred tradition to a higher level, transforming old conceptions into a new and sublime world of thought.

It was, however, especially in the XI century that the Madonna cult reached a new summit. The destruction of the world having been prophesied for the year 1000 A.D., the whole of Christendom lived in awe and fear until that year. But as the fatal date passed safely, the Christian world breathed freely again. The world's salvation, ascribed to the Virgin, "advocata nostra", "mediatrix optima", the "woman without sin" (in contrast to Eve, who originated sin), became a turning-point, and the Adoration of the Virgin began to play an important part in the pious devotions of the Church. Since that time, in the XI and XII centuries, Byzantine Madonnas performing miracles, were brought to Western Europe, taking the place of idols long since vanished but not totally forgotten, representing the black goddess of ancient times.

The Madonna in the shrine on the rocks above the river Vézère, mounting solitary guard over mankind's buried past, bears testimony to the immortality of true faith.

CHAPTER IV

THE CAVE-DEMON

1. THE WORLD OF MAGIC

The oldest history of mankind cannot be investigated by studying written documents, but can only be understood by collecting the few remains the first human beings have left behind in the places where they once dwelt. In the course of time much has disappeared entirely, and only what could resist the wear and tear of time, such as stone implements and bones, can be used to call to mind the life of those early representatives of primitive man.

Few as these remains are and difficult to interpret, they are nevertheless enough to give us a rough sketch of primitive man's doings. We can picture him hunting wild animals, gathering seed from wild plants, dwelling in sheltered places or—if in the open—screened against the wind. We have, moreover, the results of ethnological investigation for comparison as regards the life of primitive people still living. Palaeontology and geology are helping us immensely to complete the picture of early life. For these reasons we can say that we have today more than a vague idea about the body and mind of those first human beings who lived about 50,000 years ago.

Mental development had already attained to a fairly high level in what is called the "Late Palaeolithic Age". Man tried to explain to himself in some way or other the forces of nature and the mutual connection between the events he saw around him. As he belonged to, and was a representative of *homo sapiens*, he tried to detect the relation between things, for he sought to conquer the world he was living in. He wanted above all to understand the relation of his own self to this outside world. He saw himself as a part of that world, not as a subject in contrast with the world as an object, but as a subject among many other subjects with which the world is built up—a human being among a multitude of other beings, each of them with sensations, feelings and emotions he himself was aware of in his own heart. For him there were no inanimate objects, but living beings only. By means of his senses the world outside gave him an abundance of sensations, but his own inside world, his thoughts, his emotions and sentiments were so closely connected with it that the two worlds merged into each other. (16)

The recognition of this state of mind, where object and subject are blended into a single thing, is essential for the understanding of the psyche of primitives, children and artists; and some persons suffering from mental diseases fall back into this phase by means of the mental process called "regression". They are all dwelling constantly on the borderland of fact and fancy, living in both worlds at the same time.

> "The lunatic, the lover and the poet
> Are of imagination all compact,"

as Shakespeare says in A Midsummer Night's Dream.

In a mind chiefly built up from a world of thoughts like these, relations as between cause and effect are understood otherwise than in a mind where subject and object are more separate. Logos and Ratio do not take the lead when resolutions are to be formed, but the primitive tries to influence the processes of nature by "heterological" thinking. He creates a world for himself in which he is omnipotent; for this is the world where Magic reigns. He settles conflicts, fulfils his wishes, conquers the world in a way we call irrational. Nevertheless this irrational world was real enough to palaeolithic man. In fact it was a powerful means to maintain his existence in a wholly hostile world. For that it was, in the Old Stone Age.

Magic ruled the mind of those early representatives of mankind. A multitude of nature forces had to be conquered and they could be influenced and controlled by magic; not only men, animals and plants, but even lifeless objects. If the right magical procedure could be practised, the effect was ensured. Some things had to be done, others to be avoided at all costs; if they were done or avoided in the right way success was certain. Not prayers for help and happiness, but commands and exhortations for rain, fecundity and successful hunting.

A most vital question was how to use the prescriptions of magic, how to apply the magical power correctly, how to know exactly what to do and what not to do. The balance of the forces of nature is unstable, and an insignificant or accidental deviation may disturb everything, and spell disaster. So primitive man's doings and dealings were surrounded by danger, and his mind was constantly haunted by taboos.

The laws of taboo are handed down to posterity from generation
to generation, jealously guarded as secret knowledge by a few. Such
a one is the magician, the medicine-man, the sorcerer. He knows how
to increase the fertility of the wild herd, how to kill a distant foe
and how to perform the rites of transition from youth into manhood.

He must have been a mighty man among his tribe, but by no means
a ruler for the benefit of his fellow-men. He would take advantage
of his powers, claiming part of the hunting-spoils, securing the best
venison, demanding a new-made axe or the fresh hide of the animals
killed—in short, he would try to get every advantage he could,
turning his aid to good account.

Moreover, it was hard to get access to him, for he practised his
sorcery mostly in out-of-the-way places, hidden from spying eyes.
He would make his home in a cave which was difficult and sometimes dangerous to enter. There he would sit in mysterious darkness surrounded by, or dressed in awe-inspiring symbols, of his black
magic. People would approach him in fear and terror, for all who
called in his aid dreaded his anger and malice. But they had to, for
the world in which early man lived was a most dangerous one. He
had only his cunning brain with which to combat the inhospitable climate of the glacial period; his acute senses to fight the many ferocious
and savage animals that he hunted, or was hunted by in his turn, his
dexterous hands to make his axe and spear, and, last but not least, his
magic and his firm belief that, with this, he could rule the universe.
He managed to maintain his positon under the most unfavourable
circumstances in which he would otherwise have perished. He escaped
annihilation only by a sheer miracle.

2. THE HOME OF THE SORCERER

The centre of Europa in those remote times of the Late Palaeolithic Age, was totally different in respect to climate, fauna and flora
from what it is today.

The climate was very cold and the landscape was like that of the
north of Norway in our day: no forests, but chiefly tundra and
barren plains. The prehistoric man of the glacial period (for that is
the period of the Old Stone Age) at the dawn of mankind, was very
primitive. No aborigines of Australia of our time are so primitive
as those early Europeans were. They were hunters, and had few tools

and implements, for they hunted the reindeer, the bison, the wild horse, the hairy mammoth, the deer, the wolf, the cave-lion, the cave-bear, and other animals.

The earth, always covered with snow in winter, and even in summer windy and bleak, was not a comfortable place to make a home in. The people looked for shelter in the numerous caves; life was very hard and food difficult to obtain.

Such caves were the real homes of the scattered family-groups, and it was there that they lived, when not hunting over the country in search of food.

Where conditions were favourable and the mountains were built of limestone-formations, "abris sous roche" and caves were found, as, for instance, in the south of France where, in the foothills of the Pyrenees, many dwelling-places of the Old Stone Age have been discovered.

As a rule such caves are very deep, and consist of a collection of gangways, narrow passages and corridors, with here and there larger rooms and halls. There are often little streams and brooklets in the centre of the path, and also pools and lakes which have to be waded in order to reach the very last hall of the cave. The walk from beginning to end is mostly a long one, and sometimes takes a couple of hours. As the cave is in absolute darkness, good lamps are essential.

Immediately behind the entrance, as a rule, is the place where the family-groups lived; the cooking-place, the primitive implements and weapons and the bones of deer, bears and so on, are to be found there in the soil. These remains of primitive culture are also to be seen deeper into the cave.

But soon you come upon such narrow passages that it is very difficult to proceed. You have to wring yourself through openings and holes where it would seem impossible for the average man to pass. But at last, sometimes after laborious scrambling in the darkness and wringing oneself between stalactites and stalagmites, the last hall of all is reached.

In these caves, deep in the mountain, you will invariably pass here and there, pictures of wild animals on the walls, corresponding to the fauna of the palaeolithic climate, animals now quite extinct in Europe. But, as a rule, the very last hall contains the most beautiful and most numerous pictures. There may be, in fact, an entire Noah's Ark pictured on the wall (fig. 13).

This earliest human art is realistic to such a degree that we can still recognize the different kinds of bison, deer, horses, and other animals, the bones of which are to be found in the soil of the cave itself. This art of palaeolithic man is highly remarkable. It has no resemblance to any sort of art in later times, and stands absolutely alone.

Fig. 13. Rock-wall paintings, Cave "Grotte de Niau".

It bears the features of the primitive mind, is realistic, and is in the first place the result of the keen perception of primitive man. His brain had not yet undergone any important development, and a psyche of high value had not yet been formed: thoughts and considerations of a complicated nature were as yet unborn.

When picturing some wild animal, he drew a particular one which he wanted to hunt, or which he had been hunting for many days perhaps. It is a remarkable fact that he never pictured a group of animals, but only single ones which he saw in his hunting-ground. There may sometimes be a multitude of different animals pictured on the wall, but there is never any question of a group, or a herd.

This early art cannot but be realistic, for the artist pictured nature as it really was, instead of expressing his own outlook upon it. And in this fact lies the greatness of this wonderful prehistoric art—and also its limitations. For art of this kind can never pass certain limits. It can express reality, but no more. Towards the end of the Palaeolithicum we can clearly see its decline. Realism disappeared more and more, and symbolism increased. Finally this realistic art disappeared entirely. We can observe some transitions to the symbolic art of the Neolithicum, but they are very rare. This wonderful realistic art vanished as it came, in the mist of history. Wonderful as this art is, it was not practised in spare hours as a pastime or to appeal to any aesthetic feelings. It was made in grim earnest and had a deeper aim, for it served magical purposes. It was a means to influence the hostile world, and was part of a cult, if at least we may use that word here, before the dawn of religion.

Primitives believed that an image had some magical connection with the living object. By picturing the deer that he wanted to hunt, the primitive gained power over it. He directed his spear towards the picture to strike the heart, and by colouring that place with red ochre, he let it bleed to death; or he made a clay statue of some bear, or cave-lion, and then slew it by injuring it mortally with his axe. Only then was he able to kill his game afterwards.

Thus many pictures or sculptures in the caves still show the wounds, and many decapitated clay statues have been found. This is the hunting-magic, without which no success could be obtained, and which gave the hunter the feeling of safety and courage which he needed above all else.

These pictures and statues are to be seen in many a limestone-cave in the south of France. These caves are all different in size and character, and of varying interest. There are a few tolerably easy caves where one can walk without any trouble, but there are also rather difficult and even dangerous ones.

The "Grotte de Niau", large and spacious, contains many subterranean lakes of great extent. The water is absolutely clear, and without animal life. The depth is variable, but there are places where it is ten, twenty, fifty metres or more. In the absolute stillness of this subterranean world you can hear the drip-drip of the falling drops everywhere, and the mysterious sounds of the underworld are echoed from far away. In the weird solitude and the complete darkness—only relieved by your swinging lamps—you hold your breath and undergo, in this everlasting stillness, the fearful and mysterious charm of the home of the mountain-demons of this weird domain.

The ground rises and falls; here a short scrambling ascent, there a deep descent. You have to evade pools of stagnant water and little rills flowing down from the couloirs above. Somewhere far below there must be a large lake which you cannot see in the darkness. You have to proceed carefully, lest you lose your way, or slip in the wet clay and fall into the deep lake. From time to time you can hear a stone falling, clattering through one of the many invisible couloirs above and splashing with a plump into the lake far below.

Deep in the cave and, as a rule, in the very last hall the magician had his mysterious home. Here he performed the magic ceremonies and the rites of the tribe, already inherited from its ancestors. Here also he performed the secret rites of transition from youth into manhood, corresponding with the "corroborees" of the Australian primitives of our time. Here, finally, the sorcerer worked his charm concerning the fecundity of the herds of bison and deer, the principal source of food, and his spells against the wild and dangerous carnivorous animals abounding in the country. It is, as a rule, difficult to penetrate as far as this; the entrance is secret and hidden, blocked by many difficult and dangerous obstacles. There is a particular cave, high up in the foothills of the Pyrenees, where all the hardship of mountaineering in the darkness may be experienced. This cave is called the "Trois Frères".

This particular cave was explored only a few decades ago. A heavy stone-avalanche inside the mountain obliterated the whole interior at the very beginning of the Neolithicum. There can be no doubt that only palaeolithic man penetrated so far, and lived in these mysterious halls. For many hundred of centuries no human being set eyes upon the marvels of this unknown underworld.

First there is the usual scrambling through couloirs and along gangways and galleries. Then, after perhaps an hour or so, the gangway narrows alarmingly, and at last you have to dive, feet first, into a little hole in the corner. You can scarcely move there, and you have to wriggle forward on your stomach as well as you can, with your arms tight against your body. At first you go down, but soon you come to a spot where the ground rises. You become aware how difficult it is to ascend head down, or to creep round a rectangular corner in that position! You are lucky when you reach a somewhat wider part, where you can have a rest, or change your uncomfortable position. Many places are so appallingly narrow that it takes a long time to proceed even a few yards; and these extremely oppressive gangways are sometimes as long as 80 metres.

You may come to a dead stop, for the passage has become so narrow that you are jammed hopelessly between the stalactites. For some time you have to lie on the wet loam until, by pushing and

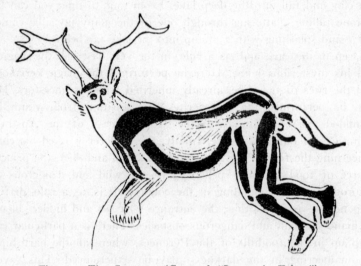

Fig. 14. The Sorcerer (Cave of "Les trois Frères").

pulling, you can free yourself from this most unwelcome and somewhat dangerous position. Only when you have passed this specially difficult gangway do you reach one of the most interesting halls ever visited in the world.

There you can find the bones, the skeletons and the traces of many cave-bears, cave-tigers, and other extinct animals, and—most surprising of all—the footprints of palaeolithic man himself, fixed in the wet soil as if he had been on the very spot a few moments before instead of many hundreds of centuries ago!

Cautiously you have to proceed, taking care not to disturb this valuable evidence of the past. After that you enter a mysterious hall

abounding with animal-pictures of all sorts, many of them bearing
the marks of mutilation with hatchets and spears.

The most startling discovery in this hall is the picture of the
sorcerer himself. Human pictures are extremely rare in palaeolithic art
and—when found—are never so clear and plain as is this remarkable
image (fig. 14).

Here you can see him in his official dress, with the antlers of a
reindeer upon his head and the skin of a cave-lion on his shoulders,
the symbols of his office; the symbols of power, fecundity and
exorcism. The image of the sorcerer is high up in the centre of the
wall, right in the middle of a great niche. From there he looks down
upon the visitor, scornful of, and angry with, the intruder who dares
to disturb the eternal rest in which he has been left since the beginning
of time. He represents the "Dieu Père" or the image of a "Saint" in
the apse of the dome of this Palaeolithic cathedral.

Only two hours later, after you have, along the same way, regained
the world of reality, daylight breaks the wondrous spell you have
undergone in the perpetual darkness of that mysterious and weird
underworld.

CHAPTER V

THE CELESTIAL CLOCK

I. CUSTOM

Medieval mind in its prime created a wonderful style wherewith to express its religious feelings. The deep-rooted emotions Christianity had aroused since it was first preached in Western Europe could not sufficiently express themselves in forms and symbols borrowed from the pagan Roman or early Romanesque epoch.

About the beginning of the second millennium A.D. the sanctuaries in Northern France were gradually rebuilt into large and spacious cathedrals of Gothic style. In the XI, XII and XIII centuries successive generations of skilful artists began to erect those marvellous buildings which we still admire today as poems carved in stone, covered with sculptures and decorations of exquisite beauty.

Though this new world of religious feeling voiced its emotions in a new language, it was nevertheless in many respects bound up with the past. For—to begin with—all those Gothic cathedrals are built on the same spot where formerly older churches stood, and where, long before our era, heathenism had also built its sanctuaries. So layer upon layer of ruins marks the place where generation after generation worshipped their gods. One can see these huge cathedrals far away, dominating the skyline of the town and overlooking the whole surrounding country. For they are all built on a prominent hill, each of them forming a veritable landmark.

There is another remarkable fact to be observed, for all these churches are built in a special direction, roughly from south-west to north-east. Even the foundations of the former buildings lie in exactly the same direction. In other words, each sanctuary was strictly oriented, and subsequent generations of architects have never altered that direction.

The question is: why did they cling to the place as well as to the orientation? Whence this custom?

With these facts in mind, let us look more closely at this problem.

The most famous cathedral in France is perhaps the Cathedral of Chartres. In its present form it dates from the XIII century, and manifests all the splendour of early Gothic style. Even today there are many fragments to be found dating from the XI and XII centuries, and on a closer examination there are even relics from much older epochs to be seen.

This imposing church is situated on the highest point of the plateau on which the city of Chartres lies, so that the building overlooks the valley of the river Eure, and dominates the surrounding country.

The history of Chartres is in fact the history of this sanctuary. When Caesar came to Gaul, Autricum (the old name of the capital of the Carnuti, i.e. Chartres, and the religious centre of Gaul) was already a famous sanctuary among the Celts, where the Druids worshipped a child-bearing virgin. So long before our era it was a place of pilgrimage whither sick persons and cripples flocked to be healed by touching the sacred statue of the Virgin.

And it is still so up to this very day. For inside the cathedral, in one of the chapels on the north side of the choir, a statue of Mary, brilliantly illuminated as it is by numerous candles, attracts the attention of the visitor. A pillar erected in front of this richly decorated image is the object of worship for the sick, who lay their hand against the pillar to receive the healing power emanating from the holy column. The history of the divine service of "la Vierge au Pillier" goes back into the mists of history, and is without any doubt associated with the original cult of this place.

The sanctuary of Chartres has often been destroyed since it was first built as a Christian church in the first century by Saint Potentein, who erected it over the ancient and sacred caves of the Druids. Gauls and Normans alike burnt and destroyed the temple in the course of time, but it has always been rebuilt with even more fascinating splendour.

The original caves where the Druids worshipped their Celtic goddess are still in existence today. The crypt of the modern cathedral contains many remains of this ancient epoch. Among them are the niches where, long before Christ, a wooden statue of a black goddess with a child was erected, on the base of which once the dedication was engraved: VIRGINI PARITURAE. The image of this "Black Mary" was destroyed by the iconoclasts and was afterwards replaced by another. The statue is situated exactly under the place where in the cathedral above "la Vierge au Pillier" stands, which facts shows how closely both are connected and how they represent the same deity. Also the altar of the ancient cult has disappeared. As a very old tradition has it both statue and altar are associated with pilgrimages before Celtic times. From the presence of a "Black Mary" we may presume that the place was sacred and taboo already before the Neolithicum.

All this may go to prove that Chartres had been a holy place from the beginning, and that successive creeds had their temples on the same spot. As an accurate investigation of the foundations of the cathedral has revealed, all these temples, one on top of the other, are oriented in the same way: exactly from south-west to north-east. Only as regards the situation of the original caves we have no information.

The cathedral of Chartres, as one of the oldest in France, is but one example out of many, for the same characteristics are to be found in other churches elsewhere in north-west Europe.

There is a more or less traditional opinion with regard to the orientation of Christian churches, viz. that the choir and the altar point towards the Holy Sepulchre at Jerusalem; in precisely the same way, as a matter of fact, as the prayer-niche (Mihrab) in Islamitic mosques is always directed towards Mecca, so that the faithful may face the tomb of Mohammed. But this opinion cannot be maintained if we observe how the axis of our churches always lies (about) south-west to north-east, and never south-east, as would be the case if the choir were directed towards the Holy Land. In this respect it is worth mentioning how the entrance of early Christian churches once faced the north-east, and the choir the south-west. In the third century, however, they were rebuilt in exactly the reverse position, which has been preserved up to our day. That first position arose in consequence of the fact that the early Christian churches were erected on the same spot, and, as a rule, with the stones and marbles of the demolished Roman temples, the doorway of which always faced the east.

The principle of orientation of churches, in fact, depends on very old traditions, the meaning of which cannot be understood without going far back into early history.

2. TRADITION

High upon the rock of the Acropolis, towering above the old city of Athens, the wonderful temple of Pallas Athena stands forth in all its beauty as the most perfect example of architectural art in the world. The wear and tear of time have not destroyed the splendour and glory of this ideal home of the gods. The illustrious history of Athens cannot be told without mentioning the fate of this, the most famous temple on record in all history: the Parthenon.

Already before the first Hellenes invaded Greece, ancient Pelasgian deities were worshipped on the Acropolis. Before Boopis Athena had been placed on the throne, Erechtheus had his home here, and a beautiful temple, the Erechtheon, treasures the memory of this "genius loci" of old. Near by is another antique temple, the Hecatompedon; and other sanctuaries stand upon the Acropolis, all dating from the time that Hellas had attained its highest culture and prosperity.

In this religious centre of Hellas it may be worth our while to look for some clue to solve the problem concerning the orientation of temples.

We know how the Persians under Xerxes in 480 B.C. destroyed all the sanctuaries on the Acropolis, and how in the time of Pericles and of his friend Phidias, the new Parthenon was rebuilt on the foundations of an older temple also dedicated to Athena. Though built on these foundations, the new Parthenon—as we know it—is nevertheless somewhat larger. But the orientation is exactly the same, so that the axis lies west-south-west to east-north-east. The temple Hecatompedon near by has the same orientation.

The entrance to the Parthenon lies on the east side, and one enters the pronaos from the east-north-east, after having ascended the flight of steps under the marvellous Doric columns. Behind the entrance is a very large hall with a stoa, and behind this in former times lay the cella, or opisthodomos, the place where, since 478 B.C., the famous statue of Pallas Athena, Phidias' masterpiece, has stood. This latter apartment, properly speaking the Holy of Holies, could only be illuminated by the doorway. It is said that on only one day of the year, the day of consecration of the god, the first rays of the rising sun shone through the entrance on to the divine statue, so that the goddess was clearly visible to the faithful who were never permitted to enter the cella. This is the traditional explanation of the fact that temples are oriented.

I do not know if this explanation holds good for every ancient temple, or indeed if most temples have been actually examined on this point. But I know of at least one temple where this conviction cannot be sustained.

This sanctuary is the temple of Apollo at Delphi. Delphi—once called the navel of the world—has always been the most sacred place in the whole of Greece, from long before the classical days of Hellas.

A very old chthonic deity was worshipped here in the form of the snake Python, son of Ge, personifying the powers of the nether world and subterranean waters and pronouncing oracles. When the Greeks came, Apollo, according to the myth, conquered the sacred place after having slain Python, took possession of the sanctuary as Apollo Pythios—and continued prophesying. The infallible oracle of Delphi is proverbial throughout the world. During the long history of Greece, from the beginning in Mycenean times until after the Roman conquest, the entire cultured world contributed to the treasuries of the temple in order to consult the prophesying priestess Pythia.

The holiness of Delphi depended originally—I am convinced—on the fountain Castalia, rising from a spring in a little canyon in Mount Phaidriades. From its subterranean waters the Pythia received her powers of prophecy. For even in the days of Apollo she used to sit in the temple on a tripod standing over the streamlet rising in the sacred Castalia spring outside the temple.

The temple of Apollo was long since destroyed and even the ruins have been removed. But the foundations, still in existence, tell a plain story as far as the orientation is concerned. The entrance opens due north-east, and in this respect there is no difference with so many other ancient temples. But if, standing on the threshold of the former pronaos, one looks eastwards, the view is completely blocked by the high rocks of Mount Phaidriades. It is therefore utterly impossible that the rising sun could ever have shone on the eastern façade and through the entrance on the divine statue of Apollo.

The orientation of this particular temple at least must have been due to some old tradition as regards temple-building in general, and is not in accordance with the facts respecting the actual environmental conditions.

We must remember that the holiness of a place may be due to

different causes. Some sanctuaries have been built over the grave of some saint, martyr or prehistoric "Old Man". Others have their origin in the healing power of some sacred spring, or are connected with sacred trees, lakes or mountains.

We shall see in the next chapter that there is indeed a definite reason why particular temples had necessarily to be oriented.

3. NECESSITY

The question of orientation in churches may be looked upon as a problem only to be solved by studying very ancient temples or, at all events, temples dating from an early period of human civilization.

A religious building certainly very striking in this respect is Stonehenge, that famous prehistoric monument on Salisbury Plain (19). As a testimony to Megalithic culture it is unique in its kind. Huge monoliths, formerly correctly arranged in circles but now fallen or missing, are witnesses to a long-forgotten past. This monument was erected by men who had but a slight knowledge of bronze and no knowledge at all of iron. From a strictly archaeological point of view it may be dated as belonging to the Early Bronze Age. But it is probable that in still earlier times, the late Neolithicum, a simpler and ruder stone circle of the same kind existed at the same place.

Stonehenge, as it is today, probably dates from 1800-1500 B.C., in a period when both stone and bronze were in use, though the latter was known as a rare substance only. Most likely it was built by a round-headed type of man, whose "round-burrows" (as Bowl-burrows, Bell-burrows and Disk-burrows) are to be found in the vicinity of the monument.

Stonehenge is only one example out of many megalithic "stone circles" once in existence in the counties of South Britain (Cornwall, Dorset, Devonshire, Somerset, Wiltshire). It is the most finished example of all, and marks the highest point of megalithic culture in Western Europe.

A most persistent tradition connects Stonehenge with Druidism. Our actual knowledge of the Druids being limited, we have only a vague idea about their religion, but we connect them as a rule with Celtic civilization. As all we know, or suppose we know, about Celtic culture is rather confusing and incomplete, it is a matter for doubt if the race who built these stone circles was not entirely different from the later Celtic inhabitants of the Plain. Megalithic culture, however, had already come to an end long before the warlike Celts invaded Britain.

Be this as it may, if the Druids were not the builders, they may nevertheless have made use of such circles—made of stone or wood— as religious monuments for worship of their gods. In this respect Stonehenge would be another example of sacred places having been built one on top of the other, and of different creeds succeeding one another and erecting their sanctuaries in the same place.

Some of the circular monuments found in South Britain were wooden buildings, as "Woodhenge", only two miles away from Stonehenge, all of which have disappeared, for the wood has, of course, decayed. Others were stone circles, which have been destroyed in the course of time; only a few are still in existence today, as for instance, at Avebury, in North Wilts. The latter is an older and ruder form, and is perhaps the prototype of Stonehenge. It was once, when perfect, one of the largest (19).

Stonehenge is certainly the most elaborate of all, and it is the only one in which the stones are wrought and provided with lintels (19). It consists of two complete stone circles: the outer one of huge megaliths of "sarsen"-stones (108 feet in diameter), the inner one of smaller "blue"-stones. Sarsen-stone is a sandstone found on Salisbury Plain, but the blue-stones are foreign, and must have been brought fom far-away Wales. Inside these two stone circles are great constructions of sarsen-stone: Trilithons, arranged in the form of a horseshoe, and inside this is another horseshoe of the foreign blue-stones. Both horseshoe-systems have their openings towards the north-east (fig. 15).

In the middle of the whole structure lies a plain slab of sandstone, called the "Altar Stone". A circular earthwork surrounds the whole Stonehenge, and an Avenue (nearly 600 yards long) bounded by earthworks, leads to the north-east.

Outside this earthwork to the north-east, and in the neighbourhood of the Avenue, stands a single crude monolith called the "Hele Stone", or "Friars Heel".

There is a great difference, and even a conflict of opinions among the scientific investigators of Stonehenge. This is chiefly with regard to the date. But we will not dwell too long here on this interesting but difficult question. It is generally agreed, however, that Stonehenge was intentionally aligned on some point of the horizon, and that the axis, lying south-west to north-east, was directed towards the rising sun at Midsummer.

This opinion is greatly strengthened by the fact that most of the stone or wooden circles in South England are oriented in quite the same way; Avebury, Woodhenge, and others, are also aligned to the north-east. At Stonehenge in particular there is overwhelming evidence of an intentional and exact alignment towards the Summer Solstice.

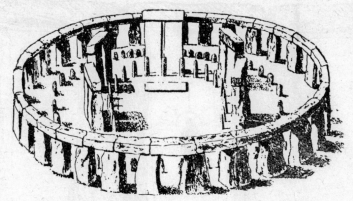

Fig. 15. Stonehenge in the Early Bronze Age.

Here we have a valuable key to the question of orientation in churches. Stonehenge, perhaps once a temple of the Sun before the age of Druidism, was never adopted by Christian people, and therefore no church or cathedral was ever erected on its ruins. We may surmise that, had this been the case, the Christian church—following the traditional orientation—would likewise have been built with the axis south-west to north-east.

We have mentioned already how the two sets of stones arranged in horse-shoe form both open to the north-east, and how the Avenue leads due north-east. But there is another and more striking fact to be mentioned. The only stone of Stonehenge that has an old traditional name is the "Hele Stone", or "Friars Heel". Seen from the centre of the monument, this stone can be used as a pointer to a spot on the horizon. It depends, of course, on the viewpoint of the spectator whereabouts on the horizon this is, but there is enough evidence to assume that the spectator had to stand on the so-called Altar Stone.

Looking from here over the top of the Hele Stone he could see the sun rise above the horizon on the day of the Summer Solstice (fig. 16).

The traditional name of this particular stone is remarkable. It is probable that the name "Hele" stone is derived from the Anglo-Saxon word 'helan", to conceal (Dutch: "helen", "heler" and "verhelen"). On the other hand, the name "Friars Heel" may be a corruption of the Celtic "cloth na freas heol", i.e. "stone of the rising

Fig. 16. Stonehenge, Midsummer Sunrise (from the Altar Stone).

sun". However this may be, this particular stone has something to do with the rising sun on a particular day of the year.

As a matter of fact the sun rises at a different place above the horizon throughout the year. In Midwinter it is farthest south, in Midsummer farthest north, nearly north-east, and it is due east on the day of the equinox. To fix a certain day of the year the day of the Summer-solstice is relatively easy to mark. As the sun rises at nearly the same spot above the horizon for several days in succession, an accurate orientation may be made to fix the exact day.

It has been the subject of serious discussion how far it would be possible to date Stonehenge by astronomical deductions. For the place on the horizon of Midsummer sunrise has varied in the course of the centuries, owing to the precession of the equinoxes. If we were able to state exactly where this place was at the time Stonehenge was built, we should be able as well to estimate the date of its origin.

This would seem to be quite easy, but there are many difficulties. First of all the variation is very slight, and the difference of a single degree means the difference of a few thousand years in dating. Furthermore, we do not know the exact place where the spectator had to stand to see the sun rise over the Hele Stone, though it is probable he stood somewhere on the Altar Stone. Moreover, many stones have fallen or have changed their position slightly, so it is difficult, if not impossible, to judge their exact position in former times. For the rest, it is a matter for doubt whether the first rays of the sun, or the fully risen sun, was aimed at.

Because the uncertainty in astronomical dating, however interesting it may be, is great, we will adhere to the archaeological date mentioned above, viz. the Early Bronze Age. Moreover, it is quite possible that there has been more than one "date", and that Stonehenge was rebuilt, or renewed, at least twice.

The main point, as far as the question of orientation is concerned, is that Stonehenge *is* indeed oriented to the Summer Solstice.

4. EX ORIENTE LUX

There can be little doubt respecting the importance of marking a special day to control the calendar and of making a correction if necessary. An imperfect measuring of the solar year must involve many confusing consequences.

We, in modern times, are accustomed to a very simple and useful calendar as compared with the past. But we seldom realize how difficult it must have been in the course of centuries to establish a really correct time-measure.

At the beginning of the Neolithicum there must have been some kind of time-measuring, for a settled community with agriculture is hardly conceivable without it. During untold ages the lunar month served as the first useful time-unit, and for a very long time the phases of the moon ruled the annual cycle. But as a lunar month has 29.53 days and a set of twelve lunar months forms a year of 354.:.36 days, there will always remain a deficit of 10.:.88 days every year. The result is that in some way or other a corrective had to be applied repeatedly to reconcile the troublesome difference, completing the year of 365 days and making the seasons agree with it.

Sooner or later every civilization has to accept a calendar based on the sun. Egypt was the first civilization which, according to Eduard Meyer, the eminent historian, established a year of 365 days already in 4241 B.C., (this so-called "oldest date" in human history, however, has been disputed lately, the year of 365 days being more probably based on the periodical Nile inundations and not on the sun). On the other hand the short-lived Maya culture never developed as far as that. The ancient Mexicans used a calendar based on the planet Venus, visible in the evening twilight during 252 days and, after having disappeared for 8 days, appearing again as the morning-star for 236 days. This very complicated calendar gave rise to many serious difficulties.

There have been many corrections of the calendar in the course of time, and even the solar year of 365 days needs a correction at fixed times to make good the loss of a single day. But the transition from the lunar year to the solar year was a tremendous and most difficult evolution, which did not pass without severe shocks.

It has been a priestly duty from the beginning to fix the dates of sacerdotal festivals and ceremonial actions. Priests were the first to study carefully the constellations of the stars, the movements of the wandering planets and the phases of the moon. Their power over the population was mainly based on their knowledge of such facts, which were guarded as holy and secret knowledge, handed down from one generation of priests to another. They were, by virtue of their sacerdotal office, the arbitrators and mediators between the divine powers and the common people.

The celestial clock, however, regulated by the phases of the moon, gains perpetually, and the dates of sacerdotal festivals would in the long run shift about. One cannot observe Christmas in the height of summer without losing something of the consecration originally connected with this holy day, nor can one celebrate a harvest-feast in Midwinter. And as these ecclesiastical ceremonies were originally bound up with the time of sowing or harvest, and closely connected with all the important actions of life—tied down to the seasons as they are—they cannot be delayed or hastened without great trouble and confusion. Anyhow, the celestial clock has to be adjusted from time to time.

When civilization developed and the scope of man spanned a wider range, when his knowledge of the motions of the heavenly bodies became more extensive, he followed the sunrise in its yearly course along the horizon. In this way he discovered the summer and winter solstices, as well as the equinox.

To his growing insight it became obvious that the sun would make a better calendar than the moon, at least if it were possible to mark the spot were the sun rises above the horizon on a special day of the year. The most suitable day for this purpose was obviously the summer-solstice.

The learned priesthood, jealously standing up for their rights, utilized this newly acquired knowledge to maintain their power. When building a temple they had merely to watch the horizon on the day that the sun rose farthest north. At sunrise the shadow of a pole, erected on the spot, would mark exactly the axis of the temple to be built. In this way the alignment of their sanctuary was fixed once and for all. On that particular day only the first rays of the sun, shining through the entrance, thenceforth illuminated the divine statue of the god, now visible to the faithful who flocked from all sides to worship the sun-god on this festal day.

I will not contend that the correction of the calendar was the only duty of the priests, or that the first temples were built for this purpose only, but I do maintain that the adjustment of the celestial clock was once the chief duty of the priesthood in the transition period from Stone Age to Bronze Age, unrivalled judges of the firmament as the priests then were.

The Sun-temple, standing high and facing the Midsummer sunrise, overlooking the eastern horizon, was therefore "oriented".

In the course of time, long after the importance of "correcting" the calendar had been totally forgotten, the tradition remained up to our day. Successive sanctuaries, dedicated to the worship of other deities, kept that orientation. It is comprehensible that Sun-temples, or such as were formerly built for this purpose, had to be oriented. They enjoyed from the first a very high esteem, and this is why other sanctuaries likewise assumed the tradition of being "oriented".

CHAPTER VI

HOW THE RAINS CAME

1. THE DANCE

For millions of years the Colorado has fretted its bed into the soil of what is now the South-West of the United States, and sent its turbulent water, laden with mud and sand, to the far-away Pacific. Nowhere in the world has a river ever furrowed out its bed so deeply as the Colorado has, whose muddy water one, when standing on the bank, can scarcely perceive a mile deep under one's feet. In the course of time it formed the most baffling object in the world, namely the "Grand Canyon". No pen or pencil has ever been able to describe or picture this marvel of beauty and splendour of ever-changing colour, line, light and shadow, on the high peaks and pyramids which form the most stupendous gorge that has been found upon our planet. To appreciate it, one must see "God's boldest and most flaming signature across earth's face".

Another world-wonder is to be found on the sandstone surface of the plateau. Here the great erosive forces of the water—at a time when the whole region was an inland sea—carried away the logs of the fallen forests that once stood on it. These logs sank with the lowering of the bottom of the sea, came to rest on their present level, and by a strange proces of nature became converted into a fallen forest of stone. This "Petrified Forest" consists of great trees of agate and jasper, and every piece of the silicified wood, polished, shows an exquisite colour hardly surpassed by any other gem in the world.

Vulcanic eruptions afterwards formed layer upon layer of lava, covering the original sandstone. Here also the erosive process has done its work, and the result of all those formidable forces of nature is that lonely landscape called the "Painted Desert".

This desert is today the home of the Red Man. In Arizona and New Mexico the aboriginal Americans are living practically under conditions already in existence before the White Man, driven by the thirst for gold, came from the south. Coronado, on his historical expedition in 1540, came from Mexico City fifteen hundred miles away, in search of the fabulous Gran Quivira, the mythical treasure town; but he departed empty-handed. Here, also, the "Seven Cities of Cibola", with their golden gates and piles of silver, were situated, whither other adventurers, as de Soto, Ponce de Leon, and Fray Marcos de Niza, travelled, drawn by the lure of gold. But what they found in the end, after great danger and hardship, was a desert, a group of adobe villages and terraced mud-houses, populated indeed by the same race that amassed the "Treasures of Montezuma", but poor savages nevertheless.

The Indian tribes now living in the basins of the Rio Grande, Rio Pecos, San Juan and Colorado, are the remnants of a vast population of tribes chiefly belonging to the Pueblo nations. The fertile valleys of the South-West, separated by expanses of desert, were once all inhabited. But long before the coming of the Whites intertribal wars and epidemic diseases had completely depopulated the towns and villages. These aboriginal communities—so-called "buried cities", though they were never buried but only abandoned—may be visited in the canyons, high up in the mountains and upon the Mesas, those typical landmarks of the South-West.

Of the Indians in this part of Arizona and New Mexico the Pueblo are the most important. Descended from the old Cliff-dwellers, they represent a very ancient stock. Once scattered all over the country in little towns and villages—each of them a republic in vest-pocket form—they have today retreated into a few pueblos (i.e. terraced community-houses) of which Taoas, Tesuque on the east Mesas, and Zuni on the west Mesas, are the best and largest representatives.

It is in the country of the west Mesas that the pueblo-tribe of the Hopi (or Moqui) lives in comparative isolation. Thus they have preserved, more than other Indian tribes, the physical characteristics and ancestral traditions of old. Their home is the Painted Desert and Petrified Forest. If one crosses the bridge over the Little Colorado from the south one enters a desert landscape, typical of the "bad lands" of Arizona. A wide horizon spans a rolling country, pathless and devoid of trees, only sage-brush growing here and there. Yonder San Francisco peak, once an active vulcano but now extinct, has covered the sandstone with lava and tufa-deposits. In the distance Shadow Mountain is seen, a black-tinted lava-hill, making the impression of being always in the shade, even in bright daylight. Before one lies the way to the pueblo Moencopi, and farther north to Tuba, the trading post. The Indian guide may draw attention to some immense foot-prints, at least two feet long, impressed in the lava at a time when it was still soft. How long ago it was since the immense animal, whose prints have been preserved up to our time, walked over this ground may be judged if one knows that these tracks are the foot-prints of some Dinosaurus, the giant reptile of the Chalk period, that, according to palaeontologists, lived about 60 millions of years ago. The tracks are as fresh as if that giant had passed here but a few days ago. This is very old country indeed!

It is not Hopi-country only. For another Indian tribe, the Navajo, also lives in this reservation. They are not a settled tribe, but wandering herdsmen and shepherds, who possess large flocks of sheep feeding on the sage-brush and other desert-plants. Great weavers they are, these Navajos. The women—for only they are experts in the art of weaving, while the men are hunters and shepherds—can be seen sitting in the open before their simple "hogan", working at their looms, and weaving those artistic designs which make Navajo rugs so much favoured by tourists. Today the two tribes live in peace, but once their tribal wars raged furiously and depopulated the country, until the American Government put an end to the troubles and settled their quarrels.

The Hopi is a farmer on a small scale. But the country is mostly desert, and the fertile valleys are few and far between. Their farming depends largely on irrigation, and above all on rain. It is indeed a matter of the utmost importance that the rains come at the right time to provide the rivers with water, to make the various grasses flourish in the Mesas, and to ripen the Indian corn in the valleys. Heavy rainfalls are followed by months devoid of moisture, and the crops are often in danger of withering away. At midday there may be a scorching temperature, especially on the desert plateau, whereas the nights are cool both in summer and winter. So the very existence of the Hopi-farmer depends chiefly on the rainfall. The question how to get rain is an extremely critical one, and a matter of anxiety for the council of chiefs of the tribe; for something has to be done to stave off disaster.

The Pueblo is profoundly religious, and deification of the mighty powers of nature—the conception of God and Nature as one—is one of the roots of his belief. Also he is by nature an artist. Religion, art and social structure are closely connected in his daily life. In the

fundamental art, the drama, the religious feelings of the primitive
are best expressed, and dancing, music, painting and sculpture are
emanations of it. It is especially in the community-dances that their
religious feeling finds powerful expression (21).

The word "dance", in this respect, has nothing to do with the
word we use for our society dances. In the rhythm of movement
and colour combined, the Indian expresses his sublime faith in the
deific order of the world.

The dance celebrates an intimate and exalted relationship with the
forces of nature, and man's mystical identification with all living
creatures in the air and forest. He dramatizes in these dances the
history of his tribe and its ancient wisdom. For the dance, like any
other art, is firmly rooted in archaic beliefs and aesthetics. Birth,
maturity, mating, death, war and peace are consecrated with community-dances. When the summer heat scorches the crops and in the
sunburnt desert the springs dry up, communication with the forces
of nature is brought about by dances. Community-dances represent
in many respects our community-prayers.

Seasonal ceremonies, having to do with the growth, ripening and
harvesting of the corn: Corn Dance, Green Corn Dance; with the
hunting of the principal game: Buffalo Dance; also with the rising
sun on special days of the year, indicating the seasons: Sun Dances;
and many others such as the Eagle Dance, the Basket Dance, etc.; all
are celebrated by rhythmic processions. Among all these the solemn
invocations for calling rain from the sky, fructifying the earth and
sustaining the life of man, are perhaps the most famous. These fervent
prayers for rain are expressed in the weird "Snake Dance" of
the Hopi.

Formerly these dances were performed in absolute isolation on the
Mesas, but today many of them are produced at the tourist centres,
such as El Tovar, on the south rim of the Grand Canyon. But to
see the Snake Dance one has to journey to the western Mesas in
the real Hopi-country.

A long series of ceremonies, performed in secret for many days
in advance, precedes the day of the Snake Dance. Late in the afternoon, when the sun goes down, two groups of priests emerge from
their respective Kivas. The Kiva, a circular subterranean sanctuary,
is the most holy place of the whole community, and it plays an
important part in every religious act of the tribe. It is also a tribal

and clan council-chamber, only accessible through an opening in the roof, and has no windows, so that the interior is illuminated only by this roof-entrance.

First the Antilope-priests, one of the two groups, dressed and painted for the ceremony, emerge from their Kiva, and form a line in front of the Kiva of the Snake-priests. After having cast some meal into the roof-opening of the Snake-kiva, they march with measured steps around the plaza. Then the Snake-priests take the stage, painted and covered with red feathers, wearing the paraphernalia of their sacred office. The chief wears a robe on which the Plumed Serpent is pictured. Both groups, facing each other, begin to hum a song, and with swaying bodies advance a few steps. Wearing arm-bands and necklaces of mussel-shells, the legs and ankles also provided with shells and rattles, they fill the air with a strange sound of song and rattle.

After some time it stops and the Snake-Priests, taking out of their Kiva a great number of snakes, all venomous reptiles—kept apart there until this moment—and handling them fearlessly, seize the writhing reptiles in their mouths, grasping the necks with their teeth.

Eevery bearer of a snake is accompanied by two helpers, one who wields a snake-whip to protect, if possible, the snake-bearer from venomous bites. Another picks up the snake if it is dropped. So trio after trio makes a circuit round the plaza amidst the excited spectators. Many a snake is dropped and tries to make its way into the surrounding crowd (fig. 17).

As the priests pass the sacred rock they are sprinkled with meal by the women standing there in line. At a given signal the snakes are thrown into a circle of sacred meal, near the rock at the corner of the plaza. The women cast the rest of the meal upon the wriggling mass of venomous reptiles, and the chief of the Snake-priests says a prayer. After that the Snake-priests grasp as many snakes as they possibly can, and carry them to the four points of the compass.

Then the dance is at an end, and women, waiting with great bowls of an emetic, give the Snake-priests to drink. These, kneeling on the edge of the cliff while the emetic takes effect, retire afterwards to their Kiva. Here they partake of as much food as is humanly possible, for the preparation of the Snake Dance has demanded many days of fasting.

Next day at sunrise the eyes of all search the sky. Thunder-clouds peep over the distant mountains of the divide. Will they come over today, or evaporate as they have done for many days in succession? A flash of lightning and a far-away clap of thunder had raised hopes during the night. Will they be fulfilled? Will the rains break through at last after the solemn dance in which the whole tribe took part?

When, at last, the sky darkens, the sun hides behind the clouds, and the long-expected rain pours down, then the river swells, the

Fig. 17. Snake Dance of the Hopi.
(drawn by W. S. Bagdatopulos, Ill. London News, Febr. 1936).

water reservoirs are gradually filled up, and the thirsty, sun-parched desert drinks in the moisture that revives it. Once more confidence in the ancient wisdom of the forbears has been strengthened—and life goes on as usual.

In picturing the Snake Dance I have followed the description by Dr. Fewkes (22), who studied the dance while it was at its best. Today Government irrigation and modern methods have ameliorated farming conditions in the Indian reservations, so that the need for rain is less felt. That is the reason why the Snake Dance—like so many other dances—is in danger of degenerating.

The Snake Dance, as a community prayer for rain, is without

doubt very ancient, handed down through untold ages from generation to generation. It is difficult to trace its origin, or to analyze the symbolism and elements of magic that form its integral parts. A conspicuous element, however, is certainly the snake as the central symbol of the whole ceremony. The "Plumed Serpent" is a familiar object in the sacred symbolism of the Indian, and widespread throughout the whole continent. Awanyu—as the Pueblos call it—is an emblem of mighty magic power.

There is evidence that the ancient Pueblo cliff-dwellers contributed many of their tribe to the people of the plateau of Mexico, the Aztecs. The legendary Aztlan (the place of origin of these emigrants) of the Aztec historians lay probably in the American South-West, and the people whence Montezuma sprang may have been of Pueblo origin. Farther south, too, to Yucatan and the Maya-people, cultural influences can be traced, and it is perhaps from there that the emblem of the Plumed Serpent, "Kukuklan" (Maya), or "Quetzalcoatl" (Aztec) came. Both Aztec and Maya worshipped the Plumed Serpent, which plays such an important part in the history of these peoples and is the source of their being called 'the People of the Serpent".

We shall deal with this interesting problem later on, but we will merely mention here that the serpent is to be regarded as a personification of the Earth. In the Snake Dance we should recognize the prayer of Mother Earth to be made fertile by the Sky-Father, by means of the Holy Water, the rain.

2. THE AXE

The parallel between the fecundation of the earth by rain from the sky, and "mating" did not escape the imagination of primitive man. At what stage of man's evolution this idea sprang up we do not know, but it must certainly have been a very early conception of his mind. It never lost its grip upon his imaginative powers, for it exists almost undiminished even up to our day.

In some way or other man tried to influence the powers of nature, for he believed he could rule the universe by magic, and in time of need or distress he had recourse to it. As the relation between cause and effect was reversible in his opinion, mating—even in a symbolic way—would effect fecundation of the earth. In the folklore of many a country we can find evidence of this opinion.

The symbolic act of mating varied, however, according to man's mental evolution. The conception of a primitive Trinity, embracing sky, earth and rain, developed in the course of time to a Celestial Father, an Earthly Mother, and Holy Water, but the symbols which were used to express the union between Heaven and Earth were not everywhere the same. In the Snake Dance we have perceived one form, but there are others as well.

An interesting form of rain-charm is to be found among the Australian aborigines in Queensland. This form of magic must once have been widespread throughout Asia, and even in Europa it can be traced in early history. But among some of the tribes in Northern Australia it is still in existence in its purest form.

The Australian aborigines are of very ancient stock, and lived for about a hundred thousand years in absolute isolation. When the Dutch, as the first white men, discovered the coast in the XVII century and went ashore to take in food and water, they found a population of primitives still living as in the Old Stone Age. These primitive savages were food-gatherers and hunters, without any knowledge of pottery or metals, wandering throughout the extensive continent in small family-groups from hunting-ground to hunting-ground, from water-hole to water-hole. Their mental development was not yet far advanced, and even now nearly all these "blackies" (as they are called today) still live in practically the same conditions. They are without doubt the most primitive men on earth.

Australia is largely a waterless country, the centre of the continent being an immense desert called the "Dead Heart", where even the aborigines can hardly live. Rain only falls sufficiently in the coastal districts, but as a rule the Australian bush is largely dry, whilst the rivers are short, many of them containing running water only in the rainy season.

The young aborigines are slender, finely built people, well-proportioned, powerful, hardy and indefatigable. Their keen senses and inherited age-long experience in the wild have made them the best trackers of all primitives, without their equals in the world. They possess but few implements, such as stone axes, long spears, wooden shields and the marvellous boomerang, that "missile that returns to its thrower". Their body is naked, only a small belt covering the hips. They live entirely in the open, at night protected only by a miserable screen. In the tropical north, in Queensland and around the Bay of Carpentaria, this may seem sufficient, but in the south the climate does not differ greatly from ours in North-West Europe; the nights are very cold in winter, and the temperature often falls far below zero.

For an everyday utensil they have only a wooden food-bowl to make dough with the meal crushed out of the seeds the women gather during the day. The only domestic animal is the dingo, a skinny pariah-dog, feeding on the refuse of the hunting-spoils.

These aborigines have a very primitive religion—if we may designate animism and magic as such—, and believe in a "hereafter" where spirits of the departed and demons frighten the living. The Wizards, old men of the tribe, enforce the rules of the many taboos by which the people are haunted. They also decide the time and place of the secret Corroborees, or Bora, and how to perform the rites of transition from youth into manhood. As far as the rain-charm is concerned, their magic expresses itself in the following interesting way.

When, in the dry monsoon, the sun out of a steel-blue sky scorches field and bush, waterholes dry up, game leaves the hunting-field in search of food elsewhere, and when a single glowing stick from a neglected kitchen-fire can set the whole country ablaze, then the council of the Old Men discuss means of meeting the coming calamity. As long as the rainy season does not commence, the tribe will suffer from hunger and thirst, women will fail to gather nourishing seeds, the infirm and the piccaninnies will fall sick and die. Starvation menaces the small family-groups, and their very existence it at stake.

Then the old tribesmen know what has to be done. Out of an age-long past they call to mind what their forbears did to escape disaster, to compel the sky to send down the pouring rain, to water the hunting-ground again.

First they built a small, primitive kind of hut of briars and shrubs wherein the ancient rite is to be prepared. Squatting round a food-bowl filled with water, muttering old magic formulas, they immerse, in profound devotion, a big stone axe in the fluid. This axe, a rough unpolished implement, which served former generations for the same purpose, has been held in high esteem from the earliest times.

Time and again the immersion of the sacred axe is performed, but the attention of the group of participants never slackens. At last they stop. Then the axe, after having done its duty, is put by with the greatest respect.

One of the old tribesmen rises solemnly. He takes the food-bowl with both his hands and, leaving the hut, he makes his appearance in the open. There he looks up to the sky as if in search of the demons who keep back the fervently desired rain. With invocations, threats, and exorcisms he calls them forth, and demands of the sky to send the rain-clouds. Swinging the water-filled food-bowl, he raises it above his head and sprinkles the drops in all directions.

Fig. 18. Rain-magic (Australia).

This is no prayer, but magic. These primitives believe that they are able to compel the sky to send down the rain, and that no demon can withstand the power of magic, rightly performed.

Axe, food-bowl and water are the elements of this performance. It is not difficult to see in the axe a symbol of virile potency and in the food-bowl—primitive precursor of the Grail!—a female receptacle. The axe, powerful weapon, killer of the foe and slayer of the game, belongs to the warrior and hunter. The food-bowl, domestic utensil to knead nourishing dough for the daily bread, is an implement for women only. The water, sprinkled in the air, represents the rain-drops pouring down. A more simple example to demonstrate the meaning of imitative magic can hardly be found.

The axe has ever since kept its reputation of bringing fertility and happiness, and became in later times an attribute of kingly power.

Such axes, made of rare and precious stone, are to be seen as "ceremonial axes" in many an ethnological museum (so for instance the wonderful specimens of Maori axes in the museum of Auckland, New Zealand). They are, as a rule, of large size, carefully polished, and

Fig. 19. Bull-head with Double Axe (Minoan).

never bear any trace of having been used for chopping purposes. Many of them, made of transparant sedimentary stone, show nebulous spots and stripes, looking like clouds and rain, and that is why tradition sometimes calls them "rain-axes". This becomes clear if we know their original use, and the way these axes once figured in the rain-drama.

We do know the axe, however, as an emblem in the fasces of Roman emperors. The Italian fasces also had the axe as symbol. We also find the "double axe" as a mighty emblem throughout the whole of Minoan culture on Crete (fig. 19), carried before the king in procession, symbolizing his sublime power. This symbol, in duplicate, formed the so-called Byzantine Cross, still to be seen in the design of military and civil orders of our day.

Among the Maori and Malayan tribes I often saw the young women wear a small stone axe as a necklace, an amulet to ensure fecundity, and a charm against evil spirits. And I am convinced that the jewelled pendants on the necklaces of our fair society ladies in evening-dress are the latter-day descendants of that ancient rain-axe, with the same background—but unconscious and forgotten.

In the mythology of many races the principal god appears as a thunder-god; for instance, Jupiter Pluvius with his thunderbolt, and Thor with his hammer. The latter was rebaptized in the Christian era as St. Olaf; but even as a Christian Saint he nevertheless retained possession of his hammer.

In the early history of the Nordic race—according to the epic Thrymskvida—the young bride was consecrated by laying Mjölnir, the Hammer, in her lap to ensure fecundity and a large family.

Thus we can still hear the echoes of a long-forgotten past, never fading completely away.

CHAPTER VII

"LITTLE BROTHER"

What shall he have that kill'd the deer?
His leather skin and horns to wear.
Then sing him home.
Take thou no scorn to wear the horn,
It was a crest ere thou wast born.
Thy father's father wore it,
And thy father bore it:
The horn, the horn, the lusty horn,
Is not a thing to laugh to scorn.
(As you like it, IV. 2.)

On the Monday following the first Sunday after Sept. 4th, a most remarkable ceremony is celebrated on the lawn before the little Parish Church of Abbots Bromley, Staffordshire, England. A small group of strangely dressed and bedecked men step from the church porch. Six of them bear enormous pairs of horns upon their heads. Among the other six (all dressed in quaint old-fashioned costumes) are two lads—one with a triangle, the other with a piece of an old cross-bow—then a man playing the part of the Hobby Horse, another as Maid Marian, then comes the Jester, and a musician with a concertina brings up the rear (fig. 20).

This is no carnival scene, but a religious procession consecrated by the Christian church and held in high esteem since time immemorial.

The horns are the antlers of reindeer, which are kept in the Hurst Chapel of the church, under the care and supervision of the Vicar himself. They may not be taken away, nor may displays of the ceremony be given outside the parish bounds.

Stepping on to the lawn the procession makes several circuits round the field. That done, the performers, still in Indian file, cross the lawn in serpentines. The men with the reindeer-horns walk in front, the others, the Merrie Makers, follow joyously, one of the boys playing the triangle, the Fool playing his roguish tricks, Hobby Horse cutting all kind of capers, and the musician playing his concertina.

After some time the participants stop walking and, forming two lines facing each other, begin a country-dance, alternately advancing and retiring with dancing-steps.

At last the ceremony is at an end, and the performers go for the afternoon and evening displays into the village streets and to the market place.

This is the "Horn Dance of Abbots Bromley", famed all over the country as a folkloristic relic.

When we saw the Horn Dance in 1934, the Rev. A. R. Ladell,

Fig. 20. Group of performers of the Horn Dance, Abbots Bromley.

M. A., Vicar of Abbots Bromley—who investigated the history of this strange ceremony in his Parish (24)—gave as his opinion that the Merrie Makers did not originally belong to the performers, but that they show the influence of the legends of Robin Hood. The dance must indeed be much older than the time of John Lackland. Also, the suggestion that the dance commemorates the granting of hunting privileges cannot be maintained. For we know for certain that before the first Normans enforced their hunting rights with the utmost severity after the Conquest, the dance was already customary.

The antlers of the reindeer are undoubtedly an important element. When, many years ago, the horns were lost in a fire, they were replaced by others specially sent from Norway for the purpose, no common deer-horns being suitable to serve in the ceremony. The reindeer has long been extinct in England, and we have to go back to the time when the last glaciers that once covered the greater part of Europe melted away, and left behind them the barren, snow-clad plains and tundras, on which Stone Age Man hunted the reindeer. In those remote times—about ten to fifteen thousand years ago— ceremonies relating to game and hunting were certainly common among the ancient hunters. But if we would try to understand what was the meaning of such dances we should have to go to other parts of the world, where the meaning of similar ceremonies is still alive in the mind of man. In Europe it is dead now. Even Christianity, the Church, could not keep it alive. At first the Church could not always wholly suppress such pagan celebrations, and had in some way or other to give compensation. It therefore sometimes adopted such festivals, gave them a Christian name, but nevertheless the original meaning was entirely forgotten in the course of time.

There has of late years been an increasing interest among American scholars in the study of ethnological facts concerning the original inhabitants of their continent, the Red Men. The school of archaeologists in the South-West, under the expert leadership of Mr. Edgar L. Hewett especially (21), has investigated the history of the Indians, excavated the old ruins, studied the uses and customs of tribes still in existence, as well as their ethics and religion. The beauty of their old ceremonies and drama-dances especially has been described by Mr. Marsden Hartley in his articles on "Red Man Ceremonies". Among other dances he also describes a hunting ceremony called the Buffalo Dance.

From what I saw myself in 1930, and from what I learned from Mr. Hartley's description, I am convinced that in many respects there is a striking resemblance between this dance and the Horn Dance of Abbots Bromley.

This dance is the most important of winter ceremonies, and is performed in every village of the Hopi. The participants, consisting of many members of the tribe and led by a man garbed as a hunter, form two rows facing each other. Between them is a woman, called the Buffalo Mother, symbolizing the mythical Mother of all animal life of the hunting-field.

Some of the dancers are masked in great buffalo-heads and faces reaching down to the breast, their bodies painted black, and their legs black and white. They are a personification of the buffalo, the principal source of animal food supply. To quote Mr. Hartley: "They bring you the sense of power of the buffalo personality, the formidable beast that once stamped the prairies around them, solemnized with austere gesturing, enveloping him with stateliness and the silence of the winter that surrounds themselves." (23).

These so-called dances—properly rhythmic processions firmly rooted in ancient wisdom—"celebrate" (according to Mr. Hewett) "exalted relationship, dependence upon deific power and gratitude for the gifts of life and well-being; stages in the progress of the individual through life, such as birth, maturity and mating; unity with all living things in forest, air and stream; humanity in its manifold activities of war and peace, of industries and art; and mythical relation with the unseen world, rich in legend and creative lore, brilliant in colour, elusive in mysticism"(21).

According to these eminent judges of the Indian mind, we have to look upon the Buffalo Dance as a ceremonial of relationship between the dancers and the animal, for it expresses the intimate relation with all life in the hunting-field. The hunter feels part of the world around him, united with his prey, incorporated into the herd on which he depends for his living, and without which he has to starve.

No individual could hunt independently. A buffalo-hunt on the great plains was a community ceremony, regularly organized, and no more animals were ever killed than necessary for daily food. After the hunt there is no show of joy, no glory about the "kill", no pride about having subdued the strong animal of the prairies.

The two mentioned hunting-dances are perhaps not the only ones, but I do not know whether more examples could be found today among other ceremonies of primitives. From what I saw of some of the dances performed by the Berber-tribes, living in the High Atlas and in the stony Sahara south of that mighty mountain-ridge, I would say that such dances must be widespread throughout that part of Africa.

The three movements of the Horn Dance are really remarkable. First the ceremonial walk around the field, no doubt in order to define the limits of the "sacred place". Then the act inside this open-air sanctuary of traversing the place in serpentines. Finally the

dance, when the two rows of performers face each other, males and
females respectively, symbolizing in this way the mating and fecundity
of the game on which they depend for their living.

As the intimate relationship with animal life is not only confined to
game in particular, but also concerns animal life in forest and air in
general, various animals—in some way or other sacred or taboo—
are the objects of worship in the ceremony. There is little doubt that
such ceremonies must be very ancient. We have curious and un-
suspected proof for this opinion in some of the works of art of the
Bushmen in South Africa.

Fig. 21. The "Mantis Dance". Mural painting at Orange Springs.

In the Kalahari, that uninhabitable desert in the south of the continent, the Bushmen lead a very poor and most miserable life as
nomadic hunters. Having long ago migrated from the north, they are
probably the last descendants of those Late Palaeolithic races once
populating Spain and the south of France. Today they are a race
dying out in most abject and wretched circumstances. But they have
inherited from their prehistoric ancestors a strong love of art, and
have left behind them on the long trail from the north those very
interesting pictures on stones and rock-walls called "Bushman
Paintings". In this marvellous and realistic art we can see not only the
game they were hunting and the way they hunted it, but even some of
the chief historic events of the tribes, which were recorded in this way.

At Orange Springs a mural painting depicts the scene of a group
of Bushmen performing a singular dance (fig. 21). Old Bushmen
testified that this is the "Mantis Dance", now obsolete, but once, when
they were youths, a sacred ceremony of their tribe. In the centre we

see five performers symbolizing the Mantis, while three others, squatting on the ground, seem to be playing musical instruments. The whole group is surounded by onlookers, men and women, applauding the performance.

This Mantis is an insect which has been the subject of legends and superstition since the day of the ancient Greeks. The name itself in Greek means "the Soothsayer", and the scientific name today is still "Mantis religiosa". In France it is called "Prie-Dieu", and throughout Southern Europe it bears different names, meaning preacher, saint, soothsayer, etc. Many tribes in Africa hold the Mantis in high esteem, and it is regarded by the Bushmen as a token of saintliness and good fortune.

But this so-called saint is, in fact, a most pugnacious insect, attacking and devouring not only its own kind, but also flies, grasshoppers, and even small frogs and birds. In China they are kept in bamboo cages to fight each other, just as the Balinese keeps his beloved fighting-cock.

It is hardly comprehensible how this ferocious insect can have become an object of veneration, except for the chance of winning money by gambling, as is mostly the case with such fighting animals. This may be the "good fortune" of the legends concerning this particular insect.

Be this as it may, it is certain that the Bushman held the Mantis in high esteem as a sacred being. It was part of his world, and in his ceremonial dances he identified himself with it.

Primitive man, in his ceremonial and rhythmic processions, dramatizes his mystic relationship with the world in which he lives. He acknowledges the inviolable ties by which he is bound up with his environment, and he tries to maintain the harmony of his inner self with nature. According to his view of life, man is not regarded as a being opposed to the outside world, but he is part of it. Always living in close connection with living things in forest, air and water, and in every way depending on the gifts of nature, he deems himself related to other beings, forming together a mystical brotherhood. The harmony of nature is unstable, and it is dangerous to disturb it. The laws of totem and taboo rule the relationship between man and this mystical world around him. Man's life is constituted by that mixture of fear and veneration so well expressed in the Latin word "sacer". Everything by which he affects his fellow-beings may in some way or other disturb the balance of nature, may bring about counter-action, harm and even calamity. He has at all costs to restore that harmony by offerings, confessing his guilt or expressing his pity. In a supreme endeavour to balance nature he solemnly identifies himself with other living beings. Thus he pretends to be a descendant of some totem-animal, the eating of the flesh of which is forbidden on penalty of death, or he imitates by solemn ceremonies the principal game on which he depends for daily food.

All this is best expressed in the moving address of a Red Indian hunter to the deer he has killed:

"I am sorry I had to kill thee, Little Brother,
But I had need of thy meat.
My children were hungry and crying for food.
Forgive me, Little Brother.
I will do honour to thy courage, thy strength and thy beauty.
See, I will hang thine horns on this tree.
I will decorate them with red streamers.
Each time I pass, I will remember thee and do honour to thy spirit.
I am sorry I had to kill thee.
Forgive me, Little Brother.
See, I smoke to thy memory,
I burn tobacco." (25).

We may, perhaps, see the last offshoot of this state of mind in the legend of the conversion of St. Hubert. For this was brought about because, hunting on Good Friday, he saw the miraculous apparition of the stag he was hunting, bearing between its horns the Holy Cross, surrounded by rays of light. Kneeling in devotion he became a faithful Christian, and, as a Saint, he is still in our days the patron-saint of hunters.

CHAPTER VIII

THE MIRACLE OF THE FIRE-WALK

They came in their frail canoes from far-away Mbengha, a small island in the archipelago of the Fiji group, to Suva on the mainland. Expert rowers as they were, they passed through the dangerous outer surf with all the skill one might expect of Polynesians who have lived in the Pacific for untold generations, people who spend their lives fishing among the blue waves of the ocean and who do not hesitate to fight—with only a knife between their teeth—that cruel monster of the deep-sea, the shark, in its own element.

When they went ashore, pushing their canoes up the sandy beach under the waving palms, their yellow-brown muscular bodies, still wet from the foam, glittered in the rays of the sun. There they unloaded from the canoes the stones specially brought from their home-land to serve the next day in the important ceremony in which the men of Mbengha would take the lead.

At the foot of a hill, near the town of Suva, the capital of the Fiji Islands, a round pit had already been dug, about five yards in diameter. The Mbengha men rolled all their stones, about the size of a football, into this pit, and covered them with trunks of trees and dry branches till the wood towered above the brink. Then an old, dignified man kindled a fire by friction, rubbing together two pieces of wood—one hard, the other soft—until a little flame sprang up which, by using a tuft of dry grass as tinder, he made greater and greater, so that it was finally sufficient to set the pile of wood in the pit ablaze.

When the smoke began to curl, and a breeze sprang up from the sea, fanning the fire, the smoking pit announced far and wide that on the next day the "miracle of the firewalk" would take place. The whole night the natives kept the fire going, and in the morning the glare of the fire-pit was visible far away, like a beacon.

The next day some of the men of Mbengha, under the leadership of the old man, who appeared to be a priest, began to build a hut of branches near the pit. In there they gathered for some time, squatting on the ground, in silence and deep meditation before the real ceremony began. In the meantime other natives armed with long poles carefully removed the charcoal and the still burning wood from the pit until the stones became visible. Some stones were turned over and arranged in such a way that they afforded a fairly steady foothold.

The heat of the glowing stones was intense enough to be felt several yards away, and dry grass, thrown into the pit, caught fire instantly. The numerous onlookers withdrew from the glare to a safe distance, or protected their eyes from the heat with their hands.

Fig. 22. Fijian Fire-walk.

At last the men in the small prayer-hut had finished their meditations and, at a sign from their priestly leader, rose from their seats on the ground. The native assistants round the pit began to chant rhythmic songs with an expectant air. The eyes of all spectators were now directed towards the few men—seven or eight in number, ceremonially dressed and wreathed,—who emerged from the hut and appeared in the open. Led by the old priest, they strode solemnly on in single file and in absolute silence, their eyes fixed unwaveringly on the fire pit. Then the onlookers held their breath, for it seemed utterly impossible that men could live in the glare and set their bare feet on the glowing stones without being severely burned.

The old priest was the first one to step over the edge of the fire-pit without any sign of hesitation; he did not even blink for a moment. Then the others followed with the same stoicism. They walked over the tottering stones and, still in single file, made several circuits within the circumference of the pit, not in the least hurried, but at every step touching the stones with their bare feet for a second (fig. 22). After perhaps two minutes, bundles of leaves and grass previously collected on the brink of the pit, were quickly scattered over the stones, covering in this way the glowing mass. On these bundles the firewalkers sat down for a while, said some prayer, and the ceremony of the fire-walk was finished.

As I witnessed the fire-walk—a very rare ceremony—in the Fiji islands in 1935, I wondered—as so many had done before me—how men could possibly walk over burning charcoal, glowing stones, or through a blazing fire, without being severely injured and blistered, or, at least, without showing painful reactions. People generally believe that the performers take some kind of precautions, dose themselves with drugs, or employ some common trick whereby the firewalk would be a simple fraud. Therefore we, i.e. two distinguished English physicians in my company and myself, took the opportunity to examine the performers before and after the fire-walk. After some palaver the native chief agreed to submit his men to this examination. Each of us selected our man— one we considered we could identify after the ceremony—and examined him carefully before and after the walk. All three of us came to the same conclusion, namely that the performers must be looked upon as normal natives; that no analgesic whatever was applied; that the men reacted normally when painful stimuli were applied to the soles of the feet or elsewhere, and that no trick whatever had been used to protect the performers from the glare of the fire. (We afterwards published these reports at home in our respective periodicals) (26).

These being the facts, the explanation of the phenomena is not a simple one. Without entering into scientific deductions, it may here be said that transient insensibility to pain and heat is well known under conditions of excitement, ecstasy and supreme emotion. The same facts may be met with during a deep hypnosis. In Indian Fakirs, under religious ecstasy and hypnotic trances, the same kind of anaesthesia may be observed. Moreover, there are many examples of phenomena like these in the history of martyrs and saints of the Christian Church, to demonstrate how religious emotion is capable of temporarily suppressing the sensibility of the skin. In all these circumstances the absence of blistering, and even of bleeding after injuries to the wounded tissue, can also be brought forward to prove how emotional life changes the normal conditions of our senses and organs.

As far as the Fijian fire-walk is concerned, there can be no doubt whatever about the religious tendency of the ceremony: the old priest leading the small group of the initiated; the meditation, introversion and prayers in the hut, preceding the fire-walk, and the tradition, still living among the Fijians, that only those who are protected by the spirits of the ancestors and the goddess of the sky are allowed to set foot unharmed on the fiery stones. Older than the memory of man, the ceremony is only performed in times of famine, when the typhoons have destroyed the crops, bananas and coconuts.

There are other islands in the Pacific, too, where this ceremony is performed—Tahiti for instance—but the fire-walk appears to have been widespread throughout the world, though now it is extremely rare. It still survives in different parts of the globe, but reports by eye-witnesses are seldom met with. Sir James George Frazer reported the ceremony in the Chinese province of Fo-Kien, and in India. There are also reports concerning the fire-walk in Japan, Mauritius, Trinidad and Bulgaria. Only lately (1936) Mr. Nio Joe Lan described the fire-walk at a Chinese temple in Java.

Though the details of the rite vary in different countries, the essential features of the ceremony are always the same. Glowing charcoal, hot stones, smouldering ashes are traversed barefoot by priests, or devotees. The rite is mostly practised near a temple, and sometimes images of some god or goddess are carried in procession through the fire. This ceremony is always closely connected with religious rites and festivals, and trances brought about by meditation and introversion of the performers invariably precede the real fire-walk. Sometimes it is a narrow trench filled with smouldering wood and charcoal, sometimes it is a round pit with heated stones and ashes, but the heat of the fire is always intense enough to blister the skin of every uninitiated man.

The origin of this strange performance being unknown, there are merely suppositions as to the meaning of the rite. Some authors associate it with spring-festivals to ensure a good harvest, or suggest that the aim is to impart by magic a sufficient degree of heat to the coming spring sunshine. If this is right, it would point to a fertility-rite, but there is little proof for this opinion.

As there is no apparent cult or deity connected with this rite, which is undoubtedly very ancient, we may presume that the fire-walk emanated from very primitive religious feelings, now nearly extinct or forgotten. We may, perhaps, surmise that the devotees have to furnish a proof of their faith by the fire-walk, and that only those who can pass through the blazing fire unharmed may be looked upon as the true believers. From this point of view the fire-walk is a real "fire-test". This fire purifies, for it selects the faithful and destroys the unbelievers.

If so, then the echo of this primitive belief can still be heard in our Christian era. For is not Purgatory the place where the Good are sifted from the Evil?

CHAPTER IX

THE MYSTICAL MARRIAGE
OF THE SERPENT AND THE BIRD

The relation between primitive man and the serpent must have been a very intimate one from the first. Earth-born and earth-bound as those first creatures were who really merited the name of human beings, they were still tied down to the soil from which—in this phase of their phylogenetic evolution—they were just raising themselves and gradually attaining the upright attitude. After having come down from the trees and emerged from the gloomy woods where their ape-like ancestors lived, they came into the open savannahs and grasslands of the semi-tropical zones. Here they developed their upper limbs—now free for the first time—into useful arms and hands, and invented the first rude implements. In search of food on the ground between the roots of plants, under stones and in waterholes, primitive man came into close contact with all the crawling and wriggling inhabitants of forest, plain and water, and among them he always met with that dangerous, treacherous and uncanny animal, the snake, abounding all around. He knew too well the effect of the venomous bite that brought a swift, silent and certain death.

Thus he associated, in awe and fear, the very soil upon which he stood and walked with the ever-menacing danger of a sudden attack from the ground under his feet, lurking in every bush, hole or pool. It struck him as a most amazing fact that the deadly power of a snake-bite was far more powerful than the mighty claws of any beast of prey. When, later on, in the course of his evolution to still higher degrees of mental development, he invented bow and arrow, he conceived the idea of utilizing snake-venom as a deadly weapon against his foes, or as a means to kill big game—which he was otherwise unable to kill—by dipping his arrow-head into snake-poison pressed out of the animal's glands.

In this way he found a powerful means to survive in his hard struggle for life. This discovery, the means to obtain and to use this kind of poison, was a most important one of primitive man's genius, for it was the great victory of man over his hostile environment, changing a fatal suspense into a means to survive [1]).

Thus the serpent, once only a dangerous enemy, became in the course of time—if handled in the right way—a helpful friend, bearing in this manner the two characteristics of every object of taboo, namely fear and hope.

This may be the reason why serpent-worship is widespread all over the globe, and in one sense or another the snake is today still part of all religions. There is indeed overwhelming evidence for the prominence of the serpent in folklore, mythology and religion. It is quite impossible to trace one's way through the very complicated and confusing mass of rites, myths, legends and religious traditions concerning serpent-worship. Perhaps no cult exists entirely devoid of serpent-symbolism in some way or other.

There are, however, some outstanding and striking characteristics to be referred to, common to all serpent-worship. One of them is the prevalence of the essential, "chthonic" character of the serpent which is indisputable even in higher religions. The serpent—or the "dragon"—represents the power of the nether world, the subterranean waters, and is associated with the healing herbs of the earth, the produce of the soil, and also with the dust unto which all men return. Thus it is the guardian of hidden treasures, it knows—because of its intimate connection with the abode of the dead—the past and the future, and it is gifted with uncanny shrewdness and wisdom.

When in the course of time the serpent, as a reptile, developed into a deity, a demon or a devil, and acquired anthropomorphic features, its original form was never totally lost, for all the gods and goddesses originating directly or indirectly from the snake, or connected with it in some way or other,—and there are a great many of them!—are always represented with some snake-emblem as an important attribute. There is, for instance, Aesculapius with a snake coiling round his staff, Pallas Athena with a snake at her feet, Kneph the Egyptian god, Krishna in India, and others. The early earth-goddess

---

1) The knowledge current among primitive peoples in our days concerning all kinds of poisonous drugs has always amazed modern scientists, who have even profited by it to utilize the healing powers of such drugs in medicinal chemicals.

in Rome, Bona Dea, had a sanctuary on the slope of the Aventine, where snakes were kept as a symbol of her medical art; Hygiea, goddess of health, was represented feeding a snake out of a saucer; the Brazen Serpent of the Bible (Num. xxi) cured the Jews of snake-bites; Siegfried bathed in the blood of the dragon and became invulnerable, and there are many other examples to prove the healing powers of the snake. And the Paradise-story (Gen. iii) bears testimony to the shrewdness of the serpent in the Garden of Eden, acquainted as the snake was with the properties of life. The Python, "son of Ge", at Delphi, was world-famed because of its knowledge of the future. In the mythology of the Nordic races, too, we can trace the serpent as, for instance, the Midgard-snake who encircled the world, and Nid-Höggr, who gnawed at the roots of the world-tree.

Many thousands of years before the art of writing was invented, and even long before mankind used hieroglyphics as a means of intercommunication, primitive symbols served to express man's thoughts and feelings. Among these symbols, as one of the most frequent, the form of the serpent can be found symbolizing "Mother Earth", the Magna Mater of later times, in this way calling to mind that very fundamental association of old between the snake and the soil.

But before continuing to trace the lot of this snake-symbol throughout the following periods, we will first deal here with another symbol predestined to become an important means of expression of human thoughts, namely the bird.

We do not know when exactly in the course of man's evolution the bird became a symbol for the sky. But it is obvious that this must have been in a relatively far advanced state of his development. It is very doubtful whether we could find with certainty one single representation of a bird among the numerous pictures of animals we know so well from the Old Stone Age. However, we do find such images on the very first pottery-fragments we know, so we may presume that in the beginning of the Neolithicum man was first in need of this symbol. When settled communities had become possible, and agriculture and cattle-rearing really began, the conditions of the weather became important facts in the life of man. He had to watch the drifting clouds and the changing winds, for the weather conditions were of great importance for the growth of crops and the breeding of cattle. For the first time man was compelled to study carefully the conditions of the sky and the changes of the weather. As a farmer, or a herdsman, he had always to keep pace with the seasons which governed his daily work. He had to recognize the portents of hailstorm, typhoon or drought if he did not wish to forfeit the results of his strenuous labour.

By attentively watching the sky, man has become aware that bird-life is always in close harmony with atmospheric conditions. Bird-life is hushed at sunset when evening is descending. Only owls and bats awake in the mysterious twilight and warn us against the dangers of darkness and night. Before sunrise the birds are the first to awake and announce the dawn; the cock especially is the herald of the coming day. When storm-clouds gather above the horizon, all birds take refuge in the trees, or look for some hiding-place. When autumn comes, birds of passage flock together and depart for the south; when spring approaches, stork and swallow are the first bearers to the north of the happy news that winter has gone and that the world is waking from its winter-sleep. It is small wonder that, more than any other bird, the cock and the swallow, as heralds of the return of the sun— whether it be a new day or a new spring—are welcomed by the people of the north as bearers of happiness, fortune and good-luck, and are therefore held in high esteem and protected and worshipped as messengers from the sun and the sky.

Thus man observed the sky, searching for signs to regulate his work with some hope of success. As he believed that such signs were sent by deities or demons of the sky, he saw in them "signs from Heaven" of approval or disapproval. Interpretation being hazardous and perhaps misleading, some specially selected men, invested with authority, were appointed to interpret these presages for the common people. We know how in Hellas and ancient Rome (up to the IV century A.D.) no military expedition, or foundation of a new colony or city was planned, or any other important decision made, without first of all consulting the flight of the birds. The members of the religious college, whose duty it was to interpret these signs, were the Auspices (auspex = avi-spex, observer of the birds), later called Augures. From the "signa ex avibus" and the "celestial auspices" they arrived at some divination, recommending an intended enterprise or dissuading from it.

In ancient Egypt some birds were worshipped from the first. Thus the oldest god, Horus, was always represented by a falcon, and performed the duty of protector to the king himself. The famous statue of Chefren (IV dynasty) represents Pharaoh with a falcon behind his head (fig. 23). In the story of the Ark the dove brought the first message that Noah's time of trial was ended. And has not man time and again awaited the coming of the "dove of peace", that fervently desired sign from Heaven?

Fig. 23. Head of Chefren (IV Dynasty, 2800 B.C.).

No further examples need here be given of how birds are believed to be messengers from the sky. Coming out of the blue, or out of dark and menacing thunder-clouds, they are looked upon as winged messengers of good or bad luck, by virtue of their supposed intimate connection with the celestial powers which control the fate of man.

Since man has tried to express his thoughts in a visible token, reducing a complex whole into a short symbol, he has used the form of a bird, or drawn merely a single wing, to indicate the Sky-Father.

What did primitive man use these symbols for? Generally not

to express his thoughts; he had a more important aim, for they served him to obtain power. By drawing a symbol or writing a word, he took possession of its object, and by naming him he acquired power over a given person. Here, indeed, there is a wide gap between primitive and modern mentality. Shakespeare's opinion:

> What's in a name! that which we call a rose
> By any other word would smell as sweet;

can never be understood by primitives. In their opinion a name is the most important part of the individual, carefully to be guarded. Therefore very often they have a secret name unknown to anyone, and are adressed in another way.

To primitive man a symbol is animated, emanating in some way or other influence and power, mostly called "mana" (a word derived from Melanesian ethnology). Being in possession of a token, a symbol, a word or a name, he acquires power over the symbolized object or the person concerned. We may, perhaps, presume that primitive man created such symbols for this purpose only. He had to maintain himself at all costs, even—if necessary—in some irrational way. He firmly believed that he could conquer nature and prevail upon his environment by magic, using the mana of drawn symbols or written words. As far as the two principal elements of livelihood were concerned, the earth and the sky, he was now able, as he thought, to compel nature to serve him.

From this point of view the pottery of the early Neolithicum is most interesting. In this same phase of evolution, when civilization began, and when in the first primitive settlements provisions had to be stored for the period between two harvests, the earliest pottery came into use. As a matter of fact, pottery and polished stone implements mark the transition between Palaeolithicum and Neolithicum.

The very first pottery fragments that we know, from Mesopotamia and Egypt, show what we usually call ornament and decoration. This fact has given rise to much speculation about aesthetic feeling as an inborn element of the human mind. But we must not forget that in this way we are looking upon the products of primitive mind from an advanced and modern point of view, and that it is very doubtful whether this opinion corresponds to the real facts. It is quite possible that early Neolithic man had an entirely different aim; for instance to protect his pottery against evil spirits, or to "charge" the contents

—consisting of precious food, seed-corn or other—with "mana". If so, then the so-called decorations were not to satisfy his aesthetic feelings, but to serve magic purposes.

If we study these early drawings and paintings from this point of view, we may ask whether it might be possible to interpret their meaning, or, in other words, to "read" them.

Neolithic art differs from Palaeolithic art by a tendency to abandon the original Old Stone Age "realism" (i.e. nature as it appears to our senses), and to accept "symbolism" (i.e. nature as we think it is). This difference, perhaps much better than any other criterion, expresses the important evolution of human mind in the long period of transition between Palaeolithicum and Neolithicum. It shows how far human mind had developed, now being able to compress a multitude of sensations into a few formulas and emblems to express its sentiments. Instead of picturing the visible world around him, man combined all this into an abbreviated symbol, fraught with meaning.

The manner in which such symbols developed in the course of time (and it must have taken a very long time indeed), was by copying time and again the original naturalistic or realistic designs, transforming them gradually, till in the long run they had lost most of their former aspect, and preserved only the essential features. In the course of time these endless repetitions became worn-out and corrupt to such a degree that the original form was hardly recognizable, until finally such a simplification came about that a single picture comprised a whole conception of ideas. We can follow this process of transformation best in the successive alterations of the human figure during the Mesolithicum and later, until at last a single mark was left in which nobody would recognize the original form (fig. 24).

This process of simplification and atrophy, in progress already long before Neolithicum began, never ceased, not even when, in later periods, realism revived here and there for a time. It called into being that remarkable geometric style, characteristic of the third and second millennium in Europe, culminating in the Dipylon style of Greece, which formed the link between Mycene and Hellas. We may find any object that could possibly be decorated—such as pottery, implements of all kind, utensils in daily use, weapons, costumes, necklaces, bracelets—covered all over with lines, curves, stripes, curls, meanders, dots, or combinations of all these. In some cases we are able to trace these elements back to the realistic design from which they originated, but as a rule we cannot go as far as that. Out of these lines and curls ornament and decoration gradually arose, tradition and convention creating a style.

But among all these geometrical designs there are still a multitude of realistic pictures to be found of men and animals (warriors, women, horses, deer, birds, lions, dogs, snakes, fishes and many others) which have not, or only partly, undergone the process of abbreviation and atrophy. A series of compositions are to be found where bird

Fig. 24. Human figures (Mesolithicum, Spain).
Transformation, simplification and atrophy of the human form.

and serpent symbols are intentionally combined in a single figure. This motive was even one of the most persistent for many centuries throughout Asia, Europe and America, and is to be found in a great many variations. Neither the bird nor the serpent have totally lost their realistic appearance, though they may have shrunk until only a wing or a single feather remains as far as the bird is concerned, and the snake became represented merely by a simple wavy line. But in spite of such reductions and simplifications there can be no doubt whatever about the interpretation of both the elements composing the symbol.

A few examples may be given here. The earliest known painted pottery was found in Western Asia, at Susa, in Elam, and dates from about 4000-3000 B.C. This is one of the places from which civilisation spread throughout the world, Egypt being the other.

Among the paintings on the pottery fragments of Susa-Elam the bird-serpent motive is frequently met with. The same combination is to

a: Susa-Elam, c. 3000 B.C.

b. Ancient Palestine, c. 1800 B.C.

Fig. 25, a-b. The Serpent-Bird symbol from pottery fragments.

be seen on the pottery of ancient Palestine culture more than a thousand years later. And when another thousand years had elapsed the same symbol was used as a prominent element of the Dipylon style in early Greece, and later also in the classic days of Hellas. These few examples may suffice to demonstrate that the bird-serpent symbol remained alive throughout antiquity (fig. 25, a-d).

c: Dipylon, c. 900 B.C.

d: Hellas, 400 B.C.

Fig. 25, c-d. The Serpent-Bird symbol from pottery fragments.

Little doubt can remain as to the meaning of this combined symbol, after all that has been said above. Man interfused two of the most potent forces of life-giving into one infinitely more powerful, for he married Mother Earth to Father Sky. With his limited knowledge and his restricted means of expressing wishes, hope and fear, he managed by this mystical marriage to create immortality. Thus he ensured fertility of the soil, increase of the herd, fecundity of the tribe and happiness for the people. In this way he summoned the perpetual succession of the seasons, and the awakening of nature in spring. In the combined symbols of the serpent and the bird we have to see the expression of a communion of hunger and starvation,

Fig. 26. Head of an Egyptian Goddess, with feather hair-dress
and serpent (XIth Dynasty, about 2100 B.C.).

as is characteristic of the primitive cultures in the early neolithic period.

When in higher cultures the belief in the king's omnipotence developed, man attributed life-giving powers to him. As the king in his divine personality combined the superhuman powers of the earth and the sky, the Pharaohs were often represented with the Falcon, as well as with the Uraeus, or cobra, around their sacred heads (fig. 26).

The history of the ancient Toltecs in Mexico is associated with the tradition of a great deity, god of the sky, called Quetzalcoatl, partly a nature-god, partly a culture-hero. He taught the people agriculture, picture-writing, and gave them the calendar. His name means Feathered Snake, or Plumed Serpent, and that is why the ancient Mexicans are called the "People of the Serpent".

There are some very remarkable parallels to be observed between ancient Egypt and ancient Mexico. The transubstantiation of the serpent-bird symbol into a living being, a mystical ruler, is one of them. In Egypt (Horus-Osiris), as well as in Mexico (Kukulcan-Quetzalcoatl), the original painted symbol developed into a culture-hero and Man-God.

The winged snake became in Roman times a symbol attributed to Mercury, god of merchants. In his staff (caduceus), consisting of two serpents twining round a staff with two wings at the top, we may surmise a symbol of his power as a protector of trade, especially of the corn-trade with Sicilia, on which the Roman Empire depended largely for its principal daily food.

This is, however, not the only offshoot resulting from the union of the serpent and the bird. This ancient life-giving symbol developed in the course of time into more complicated emblems, combined as they frequently were with more and different symbols of great power, until at last sometimes very intricate compositions resulted. And it is one of the wonders of this mystical marriage that it undoubtedly stimulated man's artistic genius, and that from this real art arose.

A few examples may be given here. A typical ornament in Egyptian architecture is the Winged Disk, symbolizing the Sun, or Sky-God, consisting of the sun-disk, falcon's wings and a couple of cobras. Almost the same ornament is to be found on lintels above the entrance of Maya temples in Central America. Though convention and tradition have changed the details of these designs, and simplification and atrophy have also done their work, the essential characteristics of the snake (head and tail) and the bird (wings) are nevertheless plainly recognizable (fig. 27). This ornament has made its way all over the globe, and in some form or other we can trace it, with all kinds of variations and under many disguises, in the decorative art of many nations and races. Though at first limited to temples and sacred places, the feathered snake nevertheless became finally secularized, transformed into scroll and garland designs of every kind. As such we may find it as a favourite ornament, a winding line with scrolls, flowers, leaves, grapes etc., in tapestry, Persian rugs, and even on our household-furniture of today. Nobody

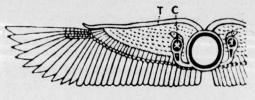

Egypt.

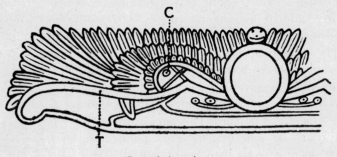

Central America.

Maya, Yucatan.

Fig. 27. Winged Disc with Falcon wings and Cobra
(C = head of the Cobra; T = tail of the Cobra).

would surmise these artistic decorations to be of holy origin (fig. 28, a-f).

The serpent-bird symbol even survives in our heraldry, for the coats-of-arms of some cities—as for instance that of the city of

The Hague, bearing a stork with a snake or "wurm" in its beak—
preserve in this way the memory of a very ancient symbol of
prosperity and good luck.

The ancient serpent-bird symbol, once of great magic power, became, when magic gave place to religion, a prayer for daily food,
as it survives in our days in the words *"Give us this day our daily*

a: Phoenician

b: Maya

c: Sivaitic (Br. India).

Fig. 28, a-c. Transformation of the Serpent-Bird symbol into scrolls and garlands.

bread", in which the exact meaning of the symbol is clearly expressed.

As a symbol it became, after almost endless conventional repetitions
—having grown stereotyped and infused with elements originally
foreign to it—in the end gradually unrecognizable; life-giving,
however, to decorative art.

This process of wear and tear has also been the fate of some prayers
as, for intsance, of that universal Tibetan prayer: "Hum Mani
Padmé Um". Though nobody knows the meaning of these un-
translatable words, they are nevertheless muttered in ceaseless mono-
tony by the adepts and devotees of Lamaism on the snow-clad plateaus
of the Himalayas, painted on the countless small flags streaming from
the poles on cairns and graves, or written on numerous pieces of paper
put into the well-known "prayer-mills" of Tibet. In the land of corrupt

d : Hellenistic, IV century tapestry.

e : Western Europe XVII century.

f : Dutch, XVIII century.

Fig. 28, d-f. Transformation of the Serpent-Bird symbol into scrolls and garlands.

Buddhism this ancient prayer has been said from time immemorial until its meaning has been lost, and it has become a senseless phrase. It only preserves the original "mana" emanating from the characters of the written words. Thus the process of decay has brought the symbol back to its original level—a process of degeneration from prayer into magic symbol. We might ask in how far some of our prayers have undergone this fate!

The story of the serpent and the bird is not restricted to religion and art only. In some myths we may also trace the influence of the union of these once so mighty conceptions of the human mind. From the myth of Perseus and Andromeda we may learn how Perseus with his winged feet, protected by a shield to which was attached the head of the Gorgon Medusa (whose hair consisted of a wriggling mass of furious and venomous snakes) rescued the maid Andromeda after having slain the dragon, which monster guarded her jealously. The usual explanation of this myth is that the sun, as Sky-God, subdues the dark powers of the nether world, and awakes the earth in spring. This myth may be the first sign of conflict between the two elements of the symbol concerned. After a long and fruitful union the snake regained its original reputation of horror, menace and danger. The first flaw in the happy marriage—preceding the divorce!

When exactly the conflict started is difficult to say. It must have been at a time when the meaning of the symbol was no more understood, its sacredness was forgotten, and its halo had faded away. The pangs of hunger were no longer felt as a continual threat in higher-developed cultures, as it has been at the dawn of civilisation.

This discord doubtless reigned a long time below the surface. An old Chinese picture (about III century B.C., fig. 29) already shows the quarrel between the two elements of the symbol, portraying a man, coming from the sky and fighting the dragon. But as far as Europe is concerned, the discord originated in the early centuries of the Christian era. A soldier of high rank, born of noble Christian parents in the reign of Diocletian, remonstrated earnestly against the pronounced hostility of the Emperor to Christianity, and his persecution of the Christians. He was arrested and martyred on the eve of the triumph of Christianity, and afterwards canonized as St. George. Legends were woven around his name, and the story of his deeds became closely associated with the legend of Perseus. According to the

"Golden Legend", St. George on his horse also slew a dragon, but in this connection there is no doubt whatever that this particular dragon symbolizes heathenism. The serpent—at last—had lost his divine glory, and became transformed into the Antichrist, the ruler of Hell.

In the reign of Edward III, St. George was made the patron-saint of England, and since that time has never ceased to fight the Antichrist.

Fig. 29. Chinese design (Honan, III century B.C.).

BIBLIOGRAPHICAL NOTE

Short list of Authors whose works supply evidence in corroboration of some of the ideas and arguments expressed in these essays, or from whose works some of the illustrations are borrowed.

CHAPTER I

1. HELMUTH TH. BOSSERT, Altkreta, 1921.
2. G. ELLIOT SMITH, Human History, 1930.
3. ——, The Ancient Egyptians and the Origin of Civilization, 1927.
4. ——, The Evolution of Man, 1927.
5. JAMES GEORGE FRAZER, The Golden Bough, 1911-15.

CHAPTER III

6. W. J. SOLLAS, Ancient Hunters, 1924.
7. O. MENGHIN, Weltgeschichte der Steinzeit, 1931.
8. JAMES GEORGE FRAZER, The Belief in Immortality and the Worship of the Dead, 1913-24.
9. ——, The Fear of the Dead in Primitive Religion, 1933-36.
10. L. J. B. BERENGER-FERAUD, Superstitions et Survivances, 1895-96.
11. P. SAINTYVES, Corpus du Folklore Préhistorique français, 1934.
12. A. S. MORIN, Le Prêtre et le Sorcier; Statistique de la Superstition, 1872.
13. TH. TREDE, Das Heidentum in der römischen Kirche, 1889-91.
14. P. E. VAN DER MEER, De taak der philosophie en de positieve wetenschap bij de studie van de cultuur van het Nabije Oosten, 1940.
15. S. FREUD, Totem und Tabu, 1913.

CHAPTER IV

16. G. VAN DER LEEUW e.a., De Godsdiensten der Wereld, 1940-41.
17. G. H. LUQUET, L'Art et la Religion des Hommes Fossiles, 1926.
18. GEORGE GRANT MACCURDY, Human Origins, 1925.

CHAPTER V

19. FRANK STEVENS, Stonehenge Today and Yesterday, 1924.
20. FRANZ BOAS, The Mind of Primitive Man, 1928.

CHAPTER VI

21. EDGAR L. HEWETT, Ancient Life in the American South-West, 1930.
22. J. WALTER FEWKES, Annual Reports. Smithsonian Miscellanous Collection.
23. MARSDEN HARTLEY, Red Man Ceremonials. Art and Archaeology (Vol. IX-XLII).

CHAPTER VII

24. A. R. LADELL, The Abbots Bromley Horn Dance, 1932.
25. ERNEST THOMSON SETON, The Gospel of the Redman, 1936.

CHAPTER VIII

26. JAMES PURVES-STEWART and DAVID WATERTON, Observations on Fijian Fire-walking, 1935.

CHAPTER IX

27. J. H. BREASTED, A History of the Ancient Egyptians, 1908.
28. ANNA ROES, Greek Geometric Art, 1933.
29. G. ELLIOT SMITH, The Evolution of the Dragon, 1920.